FATHER IN THE WILD

FATHER IN THE WILD

Dave Herring

ELM HILL

A Division of
HarperCollins Christian Publishing

www.elmhillbooks.com

Published in Nashville, Tennessee, by Elm Hill, an imprint of Thomas Nelson. Elm Hill and Thomas Nelson are registered trademarks of HarperCollins Christian Publishing, Inc.

Elm Hill titles may be purchased in bulk for educational, business, fund-raising, or sales promotional use. For information, please e-mail SpecialMarkets@ ThomasNelson.com.

Scripture quotations marked ESV are from the ESV° Bible (The Holy Bible, English Standard Version°). Copyright © 2001 by Crossway, a publishing ministry of Good News Publishers. Used by permission. All rights reserved.

Scripture quotations marked NASB are from New American Standard Bible°. Copyright © 1960, 1962, 1963, 1968, 1971, 1972, 1973, 1975, 1977, 1995 by The Lockman Foundation. Used by permission. (www.Lockman.org)

Scripture quotations marked NIV are from the Holy Bible, New International Version°, NIV°. Copyright © 1973, 1978, 1984, 2011 by Biblica, Inc.° Used by permission of Zondervan. All rights reserved worldwide. www.Zondervan.com. The "NIV" and "New International Version" are trademarks registered in the United States Patent and Trademark Office by Biblica, Inc.°

Scripture quotations marked NKJV are from the New King James Version°. © 1982 by Thomas Nelson. Used by permission. All rights reserved.

Library of Congress Cataloging-in-Publication Data

Library of Congress Control Number: 2019921100

ISBN 978-1-400330171 (Paperback)
ISBN 978-1-400330188 (eBook)

For Elijah and Marcella, from your father in the wild.

Visit fatherinthewild.com
to see the pictures and hear the songs from the story.

Contents

THINGS I USED TO HATE

"When I was a child, earth revolved at half the speed
I grew so fast to stay on top of everything
Motion was much, and stillness was rare
And I didn't care, I didn't care
I used to hate it all so much
I used to hate doing things that were no fun
I used to hate watching waves beat the shore
Things I used to hate, I don't hate anymore
Patience was a virtue that I had not possessed
Everyday was new and every new love was the best
Time was gift, and freedom was the prize
But I realized, I realized
That I used to hate it all within
I used to hate waiting for life to begin
I used to hate the surprise hid behind the door
Things I used to hate, I don't hate anymore
I was at the core of my own universe
And loneliness just made matters worse
I would lie to you, and you would call my bluff

But I grew up, I grew up
I used to hate it all so much
I used to hate it when you would show me love
I used to hate that everything can't be ignored
Things I used to hate, I don't hate anymore"

I wrote that song over a decade ago while sitting in my lonely seven-hundred-square-foot rental house in Minnesota. Everything that could have gone wrong had gone wrong that year. Well, maybe that's an exaggeration. But a lot of things went wrong. That year had driven me from extrovert to introvert very quickly, from the center of attention to the center of myself, caught up in the mess I had created. Everything I had gained throughout my early adulthood was gone overnight. The knot I had so perfectly tied only took one strategic pull of its tattered string to unravel and unwind the entire thing.

Years ago I was at a YMCA that had recently opened in my small college town, and their main attraction was a rock climbing and rappelling wall. It was nearly twenty-feet high, and you could harness yourself up and climb it. On the other end was someone holding a rope on a pulley that could easily catch and lower you down when you inevitably misstepped or slipped. My friends and I took turns attempting to scale the wall, and we all were met with the same fate each time. We all fell.

Falling by nature doesn't feel great. Our bodies weren't made to love gravitational pull. We've learned to harness that feeling in our stomachs and somehow make it enjoyable, but by nature it is our bodies' way of telling us something is wrong. I've never been a fan of falling, and it's never been enjoyable for me. I don't ride roller coasters, and you won't catch me skydiving. Keep me grounded, always.

I almost reached the top of the rock wall when I noticed that one of the carabiners that I had put my trust in during the climb was not attached. Somehow I had missed this one. It wasn't a big deal because the harness had several redundancies, but in that moment, I kind of panicked. I was nearly at the top, and my adrenaline was flowing. I took my hand off the grip to secure the carabiner, and in doing so I lost my grip with my left hand and began to fall. Luckily, my friend had the rope in his hands and he lowered me down quickly and safely. All was well.

But there was no friend holding the other end of the rope this time. It was just me.

I was a young Christian leader and I had gotten divorced. Over the course of a three-year marriage to my college girlfriend, I had become someone I didn't want to be. I hated my life, day in and day out. It wasn't her fault that I was miserable, it was my own. Misery makes you make poor decisions and not trust anyone, and pushes you into isolation. That's where I had ended up. And that's not a good place to be. So at twenty-five, our marriage ended. She moved out and restarted her life. She had pulled the string. It unraveled. It unwound.

And with no one holding the other end, I fell.

I lost my ministry and job. I lost friends. I lost a connection to my college. A line was drawn in the sand and, unfortunately, I was on the other side. To make matters worse, the recession had just hit and there was no other job to be had. I tried day in and day out to find a job. Not even a restaurant would hire me. I had to surrender to my circumstances and pack up all I had and hit the road to the one place I never wanted to return to: my family's home.

I was born in a very small town in eastern North Carolina called Kenansville. My dad's hometown was next door and that's where we lived, the city of Warsaw. But Warsaw had no hospital, though I'm sure they had veterinarians for all of the pigs. The house I was brought home to was a very small home outside of town by a few miles on a fairly well-traveled two-lane highway. It was an old block home owned by my grandfather that my mom and dad had moved into the year before when they got married. My grandfather had a small plot of land next to the house where he would farm and garden.

Every few years if I'm passing through eastern North Carolina, I try to make it a point to drive by that house. It's incredibly humble, and it's a little surreal to believe that this house is where my life began. I have no idea who I would have become had we stayed in Warsaw any longer than we did. When I drive by the house these days, it looks nearly the same as it does in my memories, which are likely tainted by photos from my early years. We moved out of that house when I was three.

Between my birth in 1983 and my graduation from high school in 2001, I lived in twenty-two different houses. I had twenty-two different bedrooms and twenty-two different living rooms. To make things more complicated, these twenty-two houses were within seven different cities. I had attended four different elementary schools, one middle school and three high schools. Stability was so incredibly foreign to me. My parents had divorced when I was ten and both remarried within a year or so. My mother had custody of my brother and I, and we had moved a few hours away from my father. We mostly saw him every couple of weeks.

As a father now, I cannot fathom what it would be like to be separated from my children. During this season of my life as a child, I remember the Friday evenings when we'd load up to go see dad. I remember getting packed for the weekend. I remember being excited.

But then there was the hour drive to the halfway point, where they would meet at a rest stop on I-40 in North Carolina. Then it was another hour back to dad's house. It made for long weekends. As a father today, I don't know how my own father did it. Or my mother for that matter. To be apart from your children is gut-wrenching. But that was the life that was tailored for us.

Since we lived with our mom, every decision she made (right or wrong) affected our life. Mom really struggled to make it for us. We moved around her hometown of Wilmington twice a year over the next five years. She had just as much trouble keeping a job as she did keeping a house. While in Wilmington, she remarried and had another child (my half brother), and things were not good in our house. It was riddled with drugs, alcohol, abuse, violence, and a lot of darkness. Her pursuit of a job eventually led us to South Carolina where things became their worst. There were times when I was in high school, particularly in this city, that we didn't even have power or running water in our home.

Eventually things leveled out, and our family became military and moved to Germany. Some things got better, many things didn't. But I eventually graduated high school and got out of there. And seven years later, as if by some divine timing or ironic fulfillment, I was returning to their house. I was moving back in with my mother and stepfather, who were now living in Colorado. Also in this season, my brothers were living at home: one home from college and the other still in middle school. It was like stepping back into time—a time I wasn't interested in returning to.

I was falling. I was living in Charlotte, North Carolina, when it all happened. My family had been relocated from Germany after seven years with the military to Fort Carson in Colorado. I had blown through all of my savings trying to survive and find a job in the recession, but I had just enough to make it to Colorado if I left soon. I planned every detail of that trip out west. I knew what kind of mileage I would get on my PT Cruiser, and I had planned where I'd stop for gas by searching for discount gas stations ahead of time. I knew it would take me multiple days, so I had joined a website called CouchSurfing, where I could stay with people for free. I knew I had to eat, so I went to the grocery store and bought three things for the drive: a loaf of bread, a jar of peanut butter, and a case of saltine crackers. I had my Nalgene water bottle I'd fill up where I could.

Since my ex-wife had moved out and we had split our belongings the way we saw fit, I didn't have much of anything to move. I put what I could into my car, which thankfully had a Thule carrier for the roof, and I put a few things at a friend's house, the only friend that hadn't abandoned me at this point. In the late spring of 2009, I pulled out of Charlotte and began the drive on I-40 west. I spent the first night in Nashville and slept at a house full of college kids I had found on CouchSurfing. They took me out that night and showed me the city. The next day I continued on through Memphis and then toward Little Rock, Arkansas. Once I passed Little Rock, I was outside of a small town called Russellville when my car turned off on the interstate. I was moving at full speed when, suddenly, the car died. The power was still on, but the engine wasn't. I had no power steering, no acceleration… nothing. I was able to safely navigate to the side of the road and attempted to start the car back up. Nothing. Over and over. Nothing every time.

I am not a hopeless person. In fact, I've always been a glass-half-full optimist. But the combination of a divorce, a job loss, a home loss, friendship loss, and then *this* was enough to cause a small breakdown.

I cursed God and shook my fist at the heavens. On the side of I-40 overlooking Lake Dardanelle, I was done with it all. It was a hot and humid day in Arkansas when even God had finally abandoned me.

Two hours later my car was towed to the nearest shop, where they told me I had a broken timing belt and the repair was going to be twenty-five hundred dollars. I didn't have any money for this. My family didn't have any money to help me. I was stranded in Russellville. My brother and mom got into their truck in Colorado to come pick me up, but it was going to be a day later. Colorado to Arkansas is a pretty serious drive, close to nine-hundred miles. I wasn't really sure what I was going to do. There was a hotel not too far away from the shop, but I didn't have money for a hotel. I couldn't sleep in my car because my car was at this small-town shop, locked up inside a garage. I wasn't sure how to sleep outside though I was considering what it would look like to try.

On a whim, I called that hotel and told the receptionist my story. I asked if they had any rooms and, if so, I could pay them within a few weeks. Not only did they give me a room that night, but one of the workers came to the shop and picked me up. It was a small glimmer of goodness on a very dark day. I didn't sleep well that night though. In fact, I barely slept at all.

There is a level of stress that comes with financial or situation problems that takes a very physical toll on your ability to rest. Even today I often need to do something to turn my brain off at bedtime, whether it's to watch a show or read. I have to do something to focus my brain to get tired, otherwise I think about a hundred things with a hundred rabbit trails to follow. I'm not even stressed really these days, and this is still my routine. Add the financial and situational stress I felt in Russellville, Arkansas, and you can understand how that night was nothing but worry and fear. Worry showed itself through anxiety as I laid in the darkness with my eyes open. Fear showed itself through the tears I was trying to fight and hold back with deep breathes to slow my racing pulse down. Every demon that has ever oppressed me was having a carnival that evening in my hotel room.

My mom and my brother showed up midmorning. They had driven all night to come rescue me. We went over to the shop and told the owner that we couldn't do the repair right now, but we'd have the car towed if he'd give us thirty days. He reluctantly agreed, and I took what I could out of my car and placed it into their truck. As we drove out of Russellville that morning, I realized that there was no returning to what I had lost. I think that before this happened, I had some belief that things would work out. Not the marriage—that was for sure over. But maybe the house would sell. Maybe friends would return. Maybe I'll get a call back from one of the thousand jobs and resumes I put out there, and I could move back to Charlotte. I had kept some hope that things would turn around and get better. It's silly to think how something as simple as losing a car could cause such a devastation and break your spirit. That car was all I had left. And I left it in Arkansas.

Late that evening, we pulled up to my mother's home in Colorado. I unloaded what I had into the spare bedroom and went to bed. It was another night of worry and fear and anxiety and tears. Worry and fear were the new theme of my life. I was the first in my family to go to college, yet I ended up living back at home only three years after I graduated.

Worry and fear always make things worse in your head than they are in reality. And the reality was that things weren't awful in Colorado. It just wasn't me. I had been on my own for seven years, and I had grown and worked through a lot of issues to become the man I had become. I would tell you today that the man I had become at that time was very broken and hurting still, but I was leaps and bounds better than I was seven years prior. And because I didn't feel at home in their house, I spent as much time out of the house as I could. I quickly found a job managing a small coffee shop/café for tourists at the foot of Pikes Peak. Thankfully there was an extra vehicle at my family's home that I was able to drive. I took that Jeep to and from work every day for twelve-hour shifts and then would spend my free time playing open mics and gigs around the entire Colorado Springs area. I had something almost every night of the week. I just never wanted to be at the house.

When I lost my job in North Carolina due to the divorce, the church I was working at did something for me that I didn't fully understand until much later. Honestly, at the time I felt very wronged by them. I was let go and never checked on. The pastors and friends who were suppose to be for me never called. They never came by. They never asked if I was ok. I felt so abandoned and hurt that no one seemed to care. As a reaction to that pain, I lashed out at them. I blasted many of them publicly on social media or any outlet I could. Pain can be a catalyst to cause pain in others, and that's very much what I was trying to do. I wanted them to hurt like I was hurting. I wanted them to be abandoned the way I felt abandoned. After all, hurt people hurt people.

I received two responses from this. One was from a pastor's wife. She rebuked me, insulted me, and basically affirmed how I was feeling. The other response was from one of the senior staff. He reached out to me and offered to send me to a place (ironically in Colorado) where pastors and church leaders can go for healing from trauma and failures or general restoration. At the time I rolled my eyes. I had no interest in going to a place to restore me into the church or ministry. I was done. I had been abandoned by God in Arkansas. It was over.

But once in Colorado, something made me feel like I needed to go. I definitely needed to get out of my mom's house for a week. I also wanted to see what could be done to get some peace from the worry and fears. I didn't want to spend the rest of my life with anxiety. I wanted to sleep at night. I wanted to be whole. I wanted to see if it was even possible to restore even a smallest part of what I had lost. A month after arriving in Colorado, I loaded up the jeep for the week and drove into the Colorado wilderness, just south of the Wyoming border on 287.

When I was a child, earth revolved at half the speed. Time goes slow when you're young. Everything felt long. The days at school felt like they went on forever, and the school year felt like an eternity. I grew so fast to stay on top of everything. I wanted to always be the leader, be ahead of everyone. I stayed on the move and didn't consider how much I left people behind. I literally moved around so many times in my childhood that I learned how to be a temporary friend and then move on. I learned how to reinvent myself with every new school or peer group I assimilated into.

I hated stillness. I hated having to wait for anything. Patience was a virtue that I had not possessed. I just wanted to keep things moving so I never had to face my realities. People were a commodity, just like time. But freedom was what I was really after. I got so used to the routine of moving and restarting that if I stayed in one city, one house, one school, or with one group too long, I had to leave them. I didn't want them to know me, and I didn't want to invest the time and heartache into others what I didn't believe I was even worth myself. I grew to hate myself for it. My heart hardened toward myself and toward others. It drove a wedge between myself and anyone else I would attempt to be close with.

I was at the core of my own universe. Even leading in the church, which is perhaps one of the most selfless things you can do, I had become so self-serving that I couldn't hide my mess anymore. It all fell apart. I lost it all. And I hated every minute of the process. That hate even projected on those I love, namely, my family. I never believed they really loved me. How could an distant father really love me? How could a mother who moved us around so much and put us in the living situations we grew up in really love me? How could my friends really love me? How could my ex-wife ever have loved me? How could my church really love me? How could God really love me?

When you fundamentally believe you're not able to be loved, the opposite begins to rise up in you, and that, my friends, is hate. It can enter your life subtly over many years through many situations and almost always through heartache. Failure to travel and explore the old roads of your life will ultimately result in a distortion of reality that you'll carry with you the rest of your days. You'll even likely project those distortions onto those close to you, whether it's your children, spouse, or friends. I want people to help me carry my burdens, but I don't want anyone carrying my pain. When I arrived at Blessings Ranch in the Colorado wilderness, I had no idea what roads were ahead of me, only the roads that were behind me. Now over a decade later, I have the same roads behind me, but a new set of roads I've traveled over the last ten years. I often like to drive the past. And I hope my drive helps you travel your own journey, as well. And hopefully you'll find some of the same things I've found and that I'm still finding, that things I used to hate, I don't hate anymore.

BEAUTY & ADVERSITY

Colorado is a very open state. There are only a handful of really populated areas, and the rest is just wide-open lands and mountains. For the longest time, it was my favorite state in the country. As I've traveled more, it's been demoted a little bit, but it's certainly still in the top five. I left Colorado Springs for Blessings Ranch and headed north toward Denver on I-25. I stayed on I-25 until I got considerably north of Denver and onto 287. Cities all look the same to me, so I wasn't paying too much attention to the drive until I got outside of Fort Collins and began heading into the wilderness.

One thing about Colorado that was evident even as I came into the state for the first time through New Mexico backroads is the abundance of antelope. They are everywhere. They were in the open fields of southern Colorado, and they are in the fields by the airport in Denver. It doesn't matter where you go in Colorado—you're going to see an antelope. As I was driving up 287, it was beautifully sunny and warm. The Jeep was incredibly loud in the wind as Jeeps are, and I decided to just embrace it and roll the windows down. Being from North Carolina, a summer without humidity is something very foreign to me. Normally you'd expect the windows down in the summertime to feel like you've gone snorkeling in the Caribbean, the way the warm wet air rolls into your car. But here in Colorado, humidity is what mothers tell children about as cautionary tales of the southeast to ensure their children stay out west. Windows down in the Coloradan summer is heaven on earth. The air is warm, but not wet. It passes over you and then back out the window. My only concern with the windows down that day was that if I hit an antelope going seventy miles per hour, it could somehow physically harm me through the open window.

As I was driving taking in the Rockies, the open lands, and the antelope, I saw something I had never seen before. There was a large coyote running along the side of the road. His tan and gray body caught my eye against the dark reds and browns of the land I was driving through. At this point in my life, I had never seen barren lands. All of the unoccupied land in the southeast is overgrown with grasses, thorns, weeds, kudzu, or anything else that wills itself to grow. It's truly evidence of the curse God gave man when He kicked him out of the garden. But here in Colorado, there are barren lands—lands with no vegetation, not even grass, just red and brown earth. 287 was a pretty good example of this. There were brush patches here and there and some grass covering in fields occasionally, but there are also stretches of the drive that are truly empty and void of any life. It's almost how I would have imagined Mars at the time. Except in Mars, I don't think there are coyotes, although I am fairly certain coyotes are a nuisance in every state in our country and possibly the world, so maybe Mars isn't a stretch.

As that coyote ran along the road, I thought about how amazing it would be if he tackled an antelope. Right place, right time. But then I quickly remembered that literally everything that could have gone wrong in my life at this point had already gone wrong, and to see a coyote pounce an antelope like something from National Geographic would likely be the equivalent of winning the Mother Earth Lottery. It wasn't going to happen for me. And it didn't. He eventually turned behind a hill and I lost sight of him. I had lost sight of many things in the months leading up to this moment. Sometimes a physical experience like this can help ground us back into the metaphysical experiences. They can help us reflect for a moment of where we are. I would never see that coyote again, and in reality, I would soon never see the man I used to be again.

We're all in a constant state of change, all the time. I think about the man I was, driving to that ranch in northern Colorado. I had an identity within me of who I believed myself to be. I knew myself and saw myself in the light of what I knew. I also had a situational identity. I was defined and identified by where I was in my life. Neither of these even acknowledge nor consider how others identify me; I'm just speaking of how I saw myself. I can tell you a few things about the man I was.

I was legalistic, theologically. I believed in a black-and-white God who didn't have a lot of tolerance or grace. I was a conservative Republican, politically. I had voted party line from eighteen to my now twenty-six. I was a musician, and I could list out my music resume pretty quickly.

And in as little time as a decade, I've all but completely shifted spectrums and paradigms. I'm pretty open-minded theologically. I acknowledge that there are black-and-white essentials in the Bible, but I don't believe there are many of them. So much is the "mystery" of it all, and it's all gray. People have been debating theological perspectives for thousands of years. Who are we to say "it is this way" for certain? Politically, I've disassociated with the Republican Party and became independent in 2016. With the way things are right now, I will likely vote democrat in the next election. While I'm still a musician, I've realized that I'm a *creative*, and there is much more to me than music. I still love and play music all the time, but I also get fulfilled through many creative outlets. And all of this is ok because changing is ok. Who I was driving down that barren road is gone forever. And even this version of myself today may look different in another ten years down the road. In fact, I'm willing to bet so much of me will continue to change.

There was no cell phone service on 287. Consequently, my phone had no GPS. I anticipated this, so I had printed directions to the ranch. They had sent directions, too, and their directions were somewhat assuming of some local knowledge, like "you'll see a grocery store, turn left and go fifty miles." I ended up finding the place about an hour and a half before sunset. I pulled in and drove quite a ways off the main road down a dirt road leading to the ranch. Once I arrived, I was greeted by the administrator and caretaker. He pointed out a house further down the road, where he told me I'd be staying with one other man who was there for the week. He suggested I go to the house, park the car, and go for a quick hike to catch the sunset. Off in the distance about a mile further down the dirt road was a small mountain called Red Nose. He shared with me that it would take about an hour to get up there from the house and that if I left quickly, I'd make it just in time for sunset. I was excited and eager to go, so I quickly dropped my things off in the house and began walking down the road toward the mountain.

It was a little strange being as far away from civilization as this ranch was. As I began walking down this dirt road, there were no cars to contend with and no houses or buildings obstructing my view. The only sounds floating through the air were the sounds of the earth. I could hear a few birds singing as they welcomed the sunset. There was the occasional rustling in the brush along the side of the road by a chipmunk. But most of that walk was met with silence and solitude. There was also the fact that I was very unprepared to hike the Colorado wilderness. The caretaker of the ranch didn't inform me of all I was going to encounter on this hike.

There was no official trail up this mountain. There was the road, but as you approach the base of the mountain, you just step off the road and start walking. There are no trees so your view is always open to where you're going, but there is incredibly thick brush that is waist high. That wouldn't have been a big deal, except I only had shorts and ankle socks with my Adidas Samba shoes. By the time I was ten feet off the road, my shoes, socks, and shorts had become covered in stick-tights, which are small seeds covered in what feels like the rough side of Velcro. And everything you wear is the soft side of Velcro. I stepped out of the brush and onto the road and spent ten minutes picking them off before I realized that I didn't just brush into a single plant that did this, rather this is basically the hitchhiker of this entire region. They are everywhere. I surrendered my will to the plant seeds and stepped back into the brush. As I moved through the brush, I kept my head and eyes down rather than up. There are two major threats I actually had been warned about.

The first was rattlesnakes. I was told they're easily disguised in the brush, but I would hear the classic rattle sound if I got too close. He did tell me that they're only aggressive if aggravated, so if I kept my eyes open and focused, I likely wouldn't have a problem. I just had to listen for the classic rattle, and if I was to hear that dreadful sound, reverse direction as quickly as possible. The other threat was cactus. This was the more pressing and obvious threat to the hike, as there was cactus everywhere. These aren't your classic saguaro cactus like you've seen in cartoons. These are small, ankle- to knee-high cactus that could easily be brushed against or stepped on.

As I walked through the brush high-stepping my way through the obstacles biting at my ankles, I started to notice there was another threat that could easily be missed. There were massive ant hills every fifty feet or so with ants the size of your knuckle. I am not a fan of bugs, especially ants. When I was a child, I had a nightmare that I fell into a swimming pool that was full of ants instead of water. I can still vividly see that dream as if it happened. It still makes me itchy just thinking about it. And these Colorado ants were huge. I began to rank the threats in my mind. First were the ants, second the cactuses, and last were the rattlesnakes.

At this point along the hike I was covered in sticktights, my bare legs had been scratched and cut up by the brush, and I've been looking down taking calculated steps watching out for ants, cactuses, and rattlesnakes. As if things couldn't get any more difficult, I came upon an old and rusted barbed wire livestock fence. It was barely too high to easily step over and too low to crawl under. It was too loose and old to stand on to climb over and too stiff to pry apart to squeeze through. I stood there assessing my options. If I tried to go over the fence, I'd likely cut myself. Actually, I was certain I'd cut myself. There were too many cactuses to go under, and the bottom wire was only a foot off the ground. Even if I could suck my entire body into my chest, I'd still get scratched by a barb or stabbed by a cactus. The option with the least risk was to try to go through it, in between the barbed wire. I was hiking with a small backpack to carry a water bottle and a few other small things I thought I may need. I removed the backpack and placed it on the other side of the fence. I made my peace with the fact that I was likely going to get scratched by this, and I thanked God that I had gotten a tetanus shot only a few years prior.

I went a few feet to my right, where there was a fence post. I figured that the post where the barded wire passed through would be tightest and most open. As I placed my hand on the post, it felt like a loose tooth. Who knows how many years this post has been standing here? The barbed wire was completely rusted over, likely decades ago. The post had stood through many freezing winters and dry summers. I didn't see any livestock anywhere, so this land was likely years or decades removed from being a practical livestock ranch. At this point my confidence for a smooth pass-through was completely gone. I grabbed the fence, spread it apart as best I could, stepped through, and pulled my body through the opening. And as predicted, a barb from the fence caught my back and marched its way across my shoulders. Thankfully, the barbs were so rusted they were hardly sharp, and it barely broke the skin.

The sun was getting lower and would soon be setting on the Rockies in the western distance. I still had a ways to go. This mountain wasn't grand by any means. Its name is only known by the locals, who named it Red Nose because the mountain was red and, well, looked like a nose. There were no trees covering it, just brush. The brush subsided at the summit, where it became smooth red rock. During the entire hike, I could see the nose of the mountain. No matter how close I got, the red nose seemed to stay just as far away. Once I reached the base of the mountain itself through a sea of brush, I began my ascent.

It was a very slow walk to the top. Loose rocks and gravel with brush slowly thinning out didn't make for a smooth hike. Not to mention I was about twenty pounds overweight, a mile high into the atmosphere on the ground alone, and walking up a very vertical and quickly rising summit. Ten steps, breathe. Ten steps, breathe. Seven steps, breathe. Five steps, breathe. This was the process to ascend Red Nose. As I was climbing up the side, behind me was a golden sun resting on the Rockies. The sunset had begun, and with every stop to breathe, I turned and faced west, looking into the golden beams of light now covering the fields and mountains of this barren land like a warm blanket. It was a lot to take in at that moment. I was standing there with miles of visibility in front of me yet couldn't see past the current crisis in my life. The dichotomy is almost ironic, especially for someone who had been in Christian leadership, which is very vision driven. I had a plan for most of my life, and I had tried to stay with the plan. I had seen things through. I had made things happen. I could see where I wanted to go, and I went.

Yet here in this season of crisis, I couldn't even see what the next month was going to look like. Truth be told, the only thing I knew that was certain about my future was that I was going to be here at Blessings Ranch for a week, and more pressing, I was about to be in the dark on a secluded mountain with ants, cactuses, and rattlesnakes. I made a final press to the top of Red Nose and walked out on the peak right in time to watch the final moments of sunset. The view from there was one of the most moving moments of my life. I could see for miles and miles to my left, right, and in front of me. Red Nose faces west, so the Rockies were on the horizon. To the south (my left) was a mountain called Steamboat, which I'm assuming is another local name to describe this small sister to Red Nose. To the north I could see the beginnings of Wyoming, the least populated state in the continental United States. Wyoming seemed familiar at that point. Isolation. Seclusion. These were the places I knew.

I caught the final light of the day as I sat on Red Nose. The sunlight washed over me, and with it came a supernatural feeling of peace. I can't explain what changed, but I can tell you something did. For the first time since my ex-wife had moved out, I felt some peace. In spite of the financial stress I was in, I felt some peace. In spite of my car sitting on a lot in Russellville, Arkansas, I felt some peace. In spite of the fact that friends I had through college and early adulthood stopped calling or checking in on me, I felt some peace. In spite of the fact that I had moved back into a house and with people I no longer really identified with, I felt some peace. In spite of losing it all, I felt some peace. I didn't do anything special. I didn't pray for anything. I just sat in the silence, taking in the beauty of the earth. God doesn't just show up when we ask. He also anticipates our needs.

Two things greatly affect the heart: beauty and adversity. Most of my life had been spent in adversity, with the six months leading to this moment being some of the greatest adversity I had ever faced. But there's something about beauty that brings peace. It gives us hope. I don't think I had ever realized how healing a moment of beauty could be until this time. And if I'm completely honest, this location or scene isn't on anyone's bucket list. In fact, only the locals know about this place. Beauty is something that is absolute *and* relative. In the absolute sense, this is a small red mountain overlooking a barren land of brush and desert in northern Colorado. It offers some spectacular views of the local area and distant views of the Rockies. I think most would agree that it's beautiful, but if you had limited resources and time, you wouldn't choose this location to go and experience. But in the relative sense, Red Nose was the most beautiful place I had ever seen in my life. I was so broken and deep in adversity. My heart was hardened to people, family, the church, and God. Beauty affected my heart greatly that day and began a healing in me that I will live in for the rest of my life.

As I reflect on my time at Red Nose that evening, I can tell you that an ancient part of me stayed up on that mountain. He did not return to the house that evening. He wasn't the one who walked along a dark road for a mile back to a small house with no television, Internet, or cell service (*today that sounds like a dream*). He wasn't the one who spent over two hours removing hundreds of sticktights from shoes, socks, shorts, shirt, backpack, and everything else they could grab onto. He wasn't the one who put eleven Band-Aids around his legs, arms, and back to cover the slowly bleeding scratches from the way the thick brush and barbed wire of Red Nose treated his body like a car wash. That part of me that had been formed since my earliest of days stayed on the mountain, and I came down with a sense of hope and newness to the days ahead of me. I laid in bed that night feeling at peace for the first time in ages.

THE RANCH

The schedule at the ranch was the same every day. I would wake up and find a simple breakfast in the house kitchen. From there, I would attend my morning session, complete morning assignments, attend my afternoon session, complete afternoon assignments, and then the entire ranch would have dinner together. There was another man staying in the ranch house with me, but I barely saw him. They alternated our schedules so we'd really only see one another at the ranch dinner every evening. I got to chat with him a little about why he was there. He too had recently gone through a divorce, and his church had sent him to the ranch for the same reasons I was there: healing and restoration. I didn't get too much of his story, honestly because I never saw him. But it was almost encouraging knowing he was there for the same reasons I was. I wasn't alone. My story had been experienced by others. It's common knowledge that nearly half of marriages end in divorce, but when you're the one going through it, it almost feels like it's never happened to anyone else. Having him there reminded me that while tragic, what I was going through was fairly common and I didn't need to feel like the only person in the world in this situation.

Morning sessions were very much focused on my story and my

need to reconcile with the hurt I had been carrying most of my life. Nearly every single day my assignments were letter writing. I wrote so many letters. I wrote to family, friends, people from my past, my ex-wife, and many people who had hurt me. These letters were never meant to be sent out, just for me to experience. I still have that stack of letters today, but I haven't read them since leaving the ranch. Maybe I never will. Writing those letters forced me to process and say the things I had been carrying for so long. Sometimes we need an assignment to force us to process our story and to say the things we've been feeling or thinking, things we've been carrying. This experience for me was the first of many steps I'd take that week. There was one letter I needed to write though that I couldn't bring myself to write. I didn't know what to say, what to feel, or what to think. I was asked to write a letter to God.

My faith journey is interesting. I don't remember my initial family going to church much. I remember some holidays in church or special events. I do remember the small country church when I was very young that basically all of my extended family attended, and I remember my grandmother teaching my Sunday school class with flannelgraphs. But after those few years of living in the blockhouse in Warsaw, I don't know if we kept attending church. I know for most of my elementary school years, we didn't attend a church that I could recall. At some point I do remember my dad getting baptized, but I don't think we attended that church often either. Everything changed when my parents divorced, though. We immediately were plugged into a church every Sunday for Sunday school and church, and every Wednesday for the dinner and programming for kids. It was a relatively large Baptist church, and it was there that I was baptized along with all of my friends. I don't remember if I had any personal faith at that point. I was just a kid, and I'm not even sure a kid can really comprehend the kind of commitment one makes to follow Jesus. I can almost say with certainty that I had no clue what I was doing and that I was just following the lead of my friends.

It was at that church for a few years that I experienced several things that shook my very young faith. I was in sixth grade when a boy brought a *Playboy* magazine to our youth group gathering, and I saw pornography for the first time. I was in seventh grade when our youth group went on a trip to a Christian music festival, and many people from our group were sitting around one evening passing around a joint. I declined, but I couldn't believe that even my friends (we were twelve years old) were smoking pot. It was later that same year in seventh grade that on a youth group ski trip, I experienced my first kiss. You can say it was poor leadership or a lack of supervision from the Youth Pastor, and maybe it was, but honestly this is what can happen when you get a bunch of teenagers together or, really, just a bunch of people. That fundamental belief that church people are less worldly, less sinful, or less hedonistic than non-church people needs to be buried as early in your faith journey as possible. Rather than learn that fact to be true, I was very shaken by it. I wasn't sure what the purpose of faith in God was if it looked just like everything else I was surrounded by.

And I know it wasn't solely the Youth Pastor's fault that I had those experiences. We switched churches when I was in eight grade and again in ninth grade, and neither youth group I was in for the next few years was any different. All of these experiences put a foundational belief in me that church was fairly meaningless. Yes, I believed in God, and I believed in Jesus. But at an early age, I wasn't sure how involved they actually were in my life or in any of our lives for that matter. Perhaps God is the clockmaker who built the clock, wound it up, and let it tick.

Occasionally He'll step back in, like He did with Jesus, to wind the clock back up and let the ticking continue.

If this is your foundational belief, then of course it's easy to feel like God isn't involved in your life, that He doesn't hear your prayers or cries for help, and that He would abandon you in Arkansas.

I started finding some real faith when we moved to Germany. I made the first friend in my entire life who was in the church and truly pursuing God with his life. He was the person I had been looking for since finding my faith. I got the feeling when I met him that he too was looking for someone who wanted to pursue God. Both he and I became really great friends for the next two years while we finished high school. We started attending a C.O.G.I.C. (Church of God in Christ) church on our military base since they had a service we thought spoke to us. I played saxophone in their gospel band, and my friend played drums. We got really involved in our base's youth ministry and started a worship band where I played guitar, he played drums, and another friend played bass. Those years were very formative to me as a Christian, and I honestly felt God was present in my life. He didn't feel like the clockmaker, but an active participant in my day-to-day life.

But that belief never rooted in me. Or if it did, the initial seed of a God who doesn't care had taken root earlier in my life, and its roots had grown deep. Now at Blessings Ranch, assigned to write God a letter, I had nothing to say because I felt like I didn't know Him. The God of my younger years (or even my prior year) was a distant memory to the God of today. I shared this story and these thoughts with the director of the ranch. He paused and went over to an old file cabinet in the corner of the room. He took out a sealed envelope, the kind you don't fold but slide your papers into, and handed it to me. He told me there was an assignment in this folder and he wanted me to complete it. He asked if I was comfortable leaving the ranch and going for a drive for a couple of hours. Of course I was. I love driving, and honestly, getting out of the ranch for a few hours sounded great. He told me of a place just across the Wyoming border he wanted me to go to, in the Medicine Bow Mountains. There's a lake there called Mirror Lake. When I'd arrive there after driving an hour and a half, I was to sit down at a picnic table, open the envelope, and complete the assignment. I grabbed some snacks for the road and a little before lunch headed northwest toward the Medicine Bow Mountains of Wyoming.

Something changes when you cross from Colorado to Wyoming. The browns and reds give way to tans and greens and a lot of open prairies. The cars on the road become much fewer. The roads seem like they are endless, and in every direction, you see the horizon. As I headed west on 130, I felt like I was driving in an ocean of grass. Being from eastern North Carolina, I've spent a lot of time at the beach. When you're standing on the shore looking at the ocean, you see water all the way to the horizon. Seeing the grass fields of Wyoming reminded me of the ocean. As I began gaining elevation and seeing snowy peaks in the distance, the landscape of Wyoming was evolving rapidly by the mile. Out of the open sea of grass were trees. There were large boulders and rocks coming up from the ground like breaching submarines. Then the mountains quickly rose and created a shoreline, with waves of snow even in the middle of July.

There was no one around, no oncoming cars, and no cars behind me. As I drove into the mountains and soon arrived at Mirror Lake, there was no one to be found. Wyoming is our tenth largest state but least populated. At only six people per square mile, you could evenly space out the entire population of Wyoming on a grid, and they would be so far away from one another that they'd be unrecognizable in the distance. While the day was sunny, it was a little windy. The mirror part of Mirror Lake wasn't really happening because the water was being blown around, causing ripples on the surface. It was still beautiful though. The entire area was beautiful. Medicine Bow isn't known for its grandeur, but its seclusion and stillness are something to behold. I'd dare say this area looks nearly identical to the way it's always looked. It's very undisturbed by people.

I found the picnic table near the lake and sat down. The assignment was to open the envelope and follow the directions. I was told to bring my Bible along, which I had done. I sat down and pulled out a two-page document from the envelope. The first page had three headings on it, and in each heading, there was a list of verses and a statement. The first heading was titled "I am accepted" and included verses like John 1:12 with the statement "I am God's child." The second heading was "I am secure" and included verses like Hebrews 4:16 and a statement that said "I can find grace and mercy in my time of need." The third heading was "I am significant" and included verses like 1 Corinthians 3:9 with the statement "I am God's co-worker."

The assignment was titled "Building a Biblical Self-Concept." My task was to go through these three headings with a total of thirty-six verses and statements and write a response to each one. One of the tenants of the Christian faith is that the Bible is the Word of God, and therefore it is true. It is a God-inspired document, and it represents truths either literally, figuratively, symbolically, poetically, or metaphorically. It is a collection of truths. To question it as a source of truth is to really abandon the core of the faith because if it is not a source of truth, then it's really has no practical purpose.

I had to square up with this thought first and foremost. Is it true?

Do I even have enough faith to believe this collection of sixty-six books, written over many generations of man from the time of Moses to 90AD, is true? I can say with doubt that it isn't. I can also say with faith that it is. I had to make a decision between doubt and faith that day before moving forward. If you logically follow the progression of doubt and faith, you arrive at the conclusion that doubt is rooted in fear while faith is rooted in hope. I had spent the last six months of my life living with worry and fear. I had just started to feel some hope for my life again. In that moment, I chose faith. I chose to believe on the basis of faith and hope alone because what I will gain from hope is greater than what I stand to lose with fear. Fear is an endless road. It's an unfulfilled appetite. It's a bottomless pit. Hope has an end. It's victory. It's rest. It's peace. And at some point in all of our lives, we're forced to reconcile between these two places: doubt and faith. This was my day of reconciliation.

I opened my Bible, and one by one with an ink pen in my awful handwriting, I wrote thirty-six responses to thirty-six statements. My responses reflected how I felt about the verse and statement. If the Bible tells me I am God's child, what kind of child have I been? If I'm one hundred percent honest, I'm not sure I've been a great child. I've been distant and shut down from my Father. I've been recluse nearly my entire life. I try to solve my problems on my own rather than allowing myself to be embraced by a loving Father. In fact, I'm not even sure I know my Father. It's interesting when we begin to connect the dots between our life's story and our faith's story. I spent most of my life projecting a lack of really knowing my biological father onto my Heavenly Father. The feelings of distance or rarely seeing my biological father transferred right over to God the Father. We know what we know. We are who we are. And if we don't take time to logically and logistically work through how we've arrived at the places we've arrived at, we're never going to fully walk in hope, in victory, in rest, and in peace.

The second page was a little different. It just had a list of verses but no heading and no statements. In this assignment, I was to read the verse and write my own statements rather than a response to the statement. There were thirteen of these verses that I read and wrote a statement to. At the bottom of the second page was a place to write a paragraph summary as a response to the assignment. Then below that, there was a place to write everything you felt in one sentence. I completed the assignment in about two hours, and then I sat on the summary and sentence for a while. I had just taken in a lot of truth about God's perception of me and all of us really—how God views people, His creation. Rather than rush the process, I placed the papers back into the envelope and started the journey back to the ranch. I got back a little before dinner, and Dr. Walker, the ranch owner and operator, asked me how it went. I shared with him that it was an incredible experience, but I wasn't sure how to summarize it.

"The letter I asked you to write to God, have you started it yet?" Dr. Walker asked.

"No, I haven't," I responded.

"Good. I want you to write a letter from God to you. What would He say to you? Use what you learned today and bring me your letter to our session in the morning."

After dinner, I went back to my room and pulled the papers out. I read through them, heard the voice of the Scriptures, and began writing.

"Dear David,

You are first and foremost my son, and I deeply love you. I will not ever leave you or abandon you. You don't have to constantly worry about people rejecting you because I will never reject you. You are free from everything that you've been afraid of, including all of your past mistakes. Know that if you confidently come to me anytime for anything, you will find grace and mercy. I creatively created you as a work of art and I have great plans for you, and you will do great things for My Kingdom. We will always work together. You are not and will never be alone. Press on. Two things greatly affect the heart: beauty and adversity. You've had plenty of adversity, now come and experience beauty.

God."

I placed my pen on the table, and I just sat and read it a few times. This was the truth I had seen in the Scriptures as I sat in the mountains. This is what God needed to tell me and what I needed to hear. Since this time, I have chased beauty. I would later marry a beautiful girl. We would travel often to beautiful places. We'd have beautiful children. I'd work with beautiful people. I'd live in a beautiful home in a beautiful city. I'd seek beauty. And don't hear this as a shallow statement of what looks good, but true beauty, which we can simply define as "goodness." The earth is full of His goodness.

LOOK TO THE EAST

E veryone likes to say that all good things come to and end, but all bad things come to an end, too. People love to say "this too shall pass" like they're quoting the poet Edward Fitzgerald, but very few people really believe the truth of that statement when they're in the "this." The "this" feels like it's the destination, as if our entire life has been leading up to "this" like a crescendo of a symphony. In the "this," hope is generally lost, and the ease of making irrational decisions is at its peak. On the darkest days that led up to living in Colorado, I believed that "this" would be my life now—that my life would be defined by failure: a failed career, a failed marriage, a failed mortgage, with all areas of life labeled with the word "failure." But that is not how the world works. Everything, even the worst of things, changes with the seasons. What was once shock and grief becomes acceptance. I had learned to accept where things were, and my time at Blessings Ranch had shown me how to rationally will my way out of where I was.

It had been some time since I left the ranch, and I had begun trying to figure out the next steps for my life. It had also been some time since the marriage ended, and everything around that situation had calmed down, just like Fitzgerald said. I wasn't receiving messages or emails anymore from nosey friends. I wasn't having a panic attack every time my phone rang, and I saw an eight-hundred number from a bill collector. Most importantly, I finally had started sleeping through the night. I've found that my quality of rest determines the clarity of my mind, and things were really starting to get clear for me.

Personally I was less than fulfilled by my daily job and routine at the cafe I was working at. I absolutely loved the location. Every day I would leave my mother's house in Fountain, Colorado, and drive up to Manitou Springs and then onto Pikes Peak. I'd hit the lower switchbacks and drive up to Crystal Reservoir to a small cafe and gift shop, where I worked four twelve-hour shifts every week, usually Monday through Thursday. And while I loved the location and didn't mind the schedule, I just didn't love working to make someone else a lot of money. I didn't feel fulfilled by that kind of work. There was definitely something missing.

I had recently started attending a church plant and was trying to get involved with them. They were small and not very good in their execution, but they provided me with some much needed community at the time. I wish I could write more about them, but honestly I wasn't involved enough with their operation to really get much past the surface. My pride made it hard to connect with them because I had come out of a situation where I was leading at a much bigger church and brought all of this great experience and ideas, ideas that they weren't interested in. For instance, their worship leader was named Chris, and he was the Lead Pastor's younger brother, right out of high school. He had no experience, and everything about the atmosphere he created (from a production standpoint) was awful. The sound was bland. The lightning was dim. Even the projector wasn't centered to the screen. Where I had worked before was a very high-detailed experience on Sunday's, and everything had to be flawless. Immediately I was distracted by all of these issues on my first Sunday.

The kid also didn't really lead with any authority. People just watched him lead the songs. Between his lack of leadership skills and knowledge of the role, I figured he'd need some help and that I could help him. I didn't personally want to be the front guy, but I loved the idea of helping him be successful behind the scenes. When I started attending, I introduced myself and told him that I was a musician and knew production. I didn't share my prior ministry experience, just that I was new in town. Immediately they plugged me into running sound or playing guitar to back up Chris. I would try to connect with him during the week, but it never worked with our schedules. I also would recommend songs and song sets that I had had great experiences leading, but they never showed up. I would offer to schedule people or communicate plans, but he never took me up on that offer, and the emails and schedule would continue hitting the band's inboxes on Saturday nights, usually around twelve hours before we were suppose to walk out on the stage.

I tried for months to interject myself upon the church's leadership team, but they never really took to me. I tried to offer my skill set and experience, but they never showed me they valued it. Eventually I started going a little less and less, responding to scheduling a little slower, and eventually, disappeared on them without even saying goodbye. It's hard to sit here today and reflect on that season because I've now been on the receiving end of that situation numerous times. A new guy shows up, brings knowledge and experience and maybe some leadership, and then expects the entire operation to respond. And every time the story plays out as if from a textbook. My story. Their story. They all end the same—gone within a few months, usually through a Houdini-style disappearance. They thought I was there and onboard, but it was an illusion. When they went to look for me in the trunk, I was already down the street. And like a street magician whom you see perform his impressive tricks and hold the crowd in the palm of their hand in one moment, I'd be gone the next day. Rather than look for another crowd to gather around me to show my tricks to, I just withdrew.

The ranch had taught me to begin to come to terms with my past and to not let the life I had lived up to that moment define me. I wasn't to let the trauma of my childhood define me. I wasn't to let the negative experiences with friendships define me, or the divorce, or the job loss. None of those things are identity markers on my soul; they're just stories and memories. Today they've become legends of old, cautionary tales for young lovers or dreamers. The stories and memories serve as various reflections in a not-so-fun house where I can look at myself and see some distorted version of me that doesn't at all square up with reality, like Christine looking into the mirror and seeing the Phantom of the Opera looking back at her. One minute you're singing and reflecting on your past and story, and the next there's a masked figure singing back to you and calling out for your trust. The ranch had taught me whose voice to trust. And I wasn't interested in hearing the voice in my head that loved to label me a victim, an ex, or a failure. Instead I was trying to find the voice of my future. I was projecting my life a year, two years, and ten years ahead and calling back to myself to give myself guidance. I would filter decisions through the future version of myself that I believed I would be and then come to conclusions that would inch me toward where I wanted to go.

You know that old saying "one step forward, two steps back?" That was my daily fear and awareness. I didn't want to fall back. I wanted to keep forward motion, no matter how small. On the hardest days, I just wanted an inch. I'd even settle for a centimeter. But on great days, I would gain feet or miles even. My enemy was never a lack of momentum, but a lack of forward momentum. I'm not one to sit still very long, so I didn't worry about becoming stagnant. I just didn't want to return to the man I was walking away from. He's selfish by nature, crafty, and manipulative. He can be very driven but driven for the wrong things. He's a guy that seems to always know the right thing for himself but makes a conscience decision to chose the wrong thing. Many people accidentally chose the wrong things in life. They make mistakes out of well intentions, confusion, or moments of weakness. Not me. I can tell you almost every way I've ever wronged myself has been my choice. And I don't mean a choice made in an irrational moment. I am calculating.

A year before things fell apart with my ex, I had written a song about my desire for hope in my life and how it always lost to my own desire for destruction. The song was called "Look to the East," and it was the title track to the first solo project I ever did. I wrote every song, recorded every song, and mixed every song. I gave almost a year of my life to that process, and "Look to the East" was the title track. In it, I said:

"Everyday I look for peace, never looking to the east
Where the sun will bring new light to face the night
Everyday I hope for love, and some blessings from above
But my eyes keep to the west because I all I want to see is darkness."

It's an odd concept to only want to see darkness. It's not something that sounds normal or natural. Even writing it on paper required me to read and reread it a few times to make sure it's making sense in my head. What I've come to realize as I've processed this concept over and over is that I want to see darkness because my default expectation is darkness. Let me put that is in less poetic terms. I've come to expect to be disappointed, to be hurt, to be betrayed, to be lied to and deceived, and to be abandoned. I've come to expect that people are simply going to do me wrong. With that foundational belief, I keep my outlook and expectations very low. It's an odd place to be. I'm a glass-half-full, optimistic, and positive person. Yet I have zero expectations in people and situations. It's a strange dichotomy to feel.

A few months after I left the church in Colorado for the last time, I realized that rather than aligning myself to their vision and mission, I was trying to bring mine to their house. It would be like walking into someone's home and telling them how to cook, clean, decorate, handle their finances, do maintenance, and all of the other things that we do in our day-to-day lives. A better position would have been to learn how they live, be known for my good character, and, when or if asked and consulted, humbly offer anything I had learned or gained through the years. That would have been a more gentle way to assimilate into that community, and gentleness is a "fruit of the Spirit."

I never went back to a church in Colorado. I spent my Sunday's out hiking or driving through the mountains, trying to connect with beauty to keep my heart stimulated. Beauty is in the eye of the beholder. One of my favorite musicians of all time, Rich Mullins, saw beauty in the church:

"And if I were a painter I do not know which I'd paint
The calling of the ancient stars or assembling of the saints…"

In this season, I couldn't see the beauty in the assembling of the saints. But I could see it in nature. I could see it in the mountains and on the prairies. There was something so profoundly spiritual about this season of my life. While I was living as an orphan from the church, I was on a journey for my Father in the wild. I'm not saying it was the right approach, or even the wise approach, but it's what I did.

Lost Springs

From Colorado, there are many accessible places of beauty that you can easily drive to. There are incredible mountain ranges in the state itself and even four National Parks. Just across the state border to the west is Utah with several more National Parks. To the north into Wyoming, you have Yellowstone and the Grand Tetons. There really is no shortage of beauty accessible from Colorado. My goal was to wrap up my time in this part of the country with a road trip to see something I'd never seen before. Something that would inspire me. Something that would move me. I started by consulting my budget, which was pretty slim. I was planning to leave Colorado in the early fall and move back to the east coast to figure things out.

But I needed something before this journey back east that wouldn't have any other agenda. With money set aside for the move, I began to calculate what it would take to go on a short journey for myself. It was a constant balance of how many miles I could cover, how many nights I'd have to plan on being away for, and how many meals I would need to be gone those many nights. The basic necessities of life are food and shelter. Balancing those with mileage, I determined that the smartest adventure that would get me the most bang for my buck was

South Dakota. I could drive north never worrying about the Rockies and how they'd affect my gas mileage. I could spend most of my drive on the backroads of Wyoming, seeing the open prairies and vast sea of grass and wheat I had seen in the months prior in the Medicine Bow Mountains. I would hit some mountains at the Black Hills and see Mount Rushmore and Custer State Park. I could see the small and historic city of Rapid City in South Dakota and easily find lodging, food, and gas. From there I would reach my final destination, the Badlands, a strange anomaly in the South Dakota prairies. Seeing this would be the highlight of the trip, and then I would head back to Colorado.

I had spent the entire summer driving my family's Jeep Wrangler in Colorado. It was perfect for the location, as I looked like a local who frequented the off-road tracks around Colorado Springs. In fact, I had many opportunities to do just that with my younger brother Daniel. The Jeep actually belonged to him, but he also had a motorcycle he drove most days. My car had been spending its summer in a lot at the repair shop in Russellville, Arkansas, where I had abandoned it a few months earlier after it had abandoned me on the side of the road. I had bought that PT Cruiser several years earlier when I was in college. I was playing a lot of music around the region and needed a large vehicle that could haul around a lot of amps and guitars. It had worked out really well for those years, as I could fold the seats up like a minivan and get anything I needed in that car. I had even bought a Thule roof carrier and racks for the roof. This car could carry a lot of stuff, and I used that space all of the time in the years it was running fine. When I bought it, the car had thirty-six thousand miles on it. Five years later on its journey to Colorado, the timing belt broke in Arkansas. It had a little over one-hundred thousand miles on it at this time. A timing belt break is a big deal. It wasn't an easy fix, nor was it inexpensive. There was also the possibility that when the belt broke, more significant damage was done to the engine. The mechanic in Russellville wasn't able to really give me clarity on this without starting the repair, and the four-digit quote for the repair was out of my reach.

The PT Cruiser (as my friends appropriately called it all of those years, the PT Loser) had been sitting for a few months in the back lot of the mechanic's shop in Arkansas, and they needed me to do something with it. I had loaded it out as much as I could when my family rescued me, so I wasn't sure what was in the car at this point. The racks and Thule carrier were still on the car. It was in great shape cosmetically and operationally as far as I knew, save the timing belt issue. I didn't want to junk it. I knew that if I could get it fixed, I would probably get a few more years out of it. I just wasn't sure what to do from Colorado.

During my time there, I had a mechanic referenced to me that was confident he could fix it on the cheap. He had repaired many PT Cruisers with the same timing belt issue and said they rarely caused any more damage. His quote, while still four digits, was half of what the guy in Arkansas quoted me. I just had to figure out how to get it back. I began searching online for car movers and car carries and connected with a guy who had a car carrier that hauled luxury vehicles around the country as wealthy people bought and sold vintage cars. He said he was going to be traveling I-40 and had a couple of open spaces on his truck through Colorado. It was a sure winning situation, and my PT Cruiser would experience an elevated social status for the first time in its loser life. The man would go to the shop in Russellville, pick up the car, and deliver it right to the shop in Colorado Springs for only a few hundred dollars. I paid the man, and a few days went by while I waited for him to call and confirm his pickup in Russellville. The day of pickup came, and he called and told me there was a problem. With the Thule carrier on the car, there was no way to get it onto his truck. He asked if I had left the key to the carrier in the car, which would have allowed him to open the carrier and remove it from the car. Unfortunately I had not left the key there, though it would have made total sense to leave the key in the glove box. I gave him the verbal go-ahead to break the lock, open the carrier, and remove it. He loaded the car into his truck and slid the carrier beside it. A few days later, he dropped the car off at the shop in Colorado.

I was able to leave work a little early the day he dropped the car off. I hadn't seen my car for months, and it had sat out in a grass lot all summer. I wasn't sure what the car was going to look like or what shape it was going to be in after those months. When I saw it, it was in decent shape for the most part. All of the tires looked like they had lost air. The car had a green grime on it that I can only describe as "the south." It definitely needed to be washed and shown a little love. The mechanic got right into it and confirmed that his quote was accurate and I could have it ready in just a few days. I was ecstatic to have my car back. I was so grateful that I had that Jeep all summer, but I missed my car. I missed how quiet it was compared to the Jeep, which was all utility. I missed having a decent stereo and speakers. I missed the gas mileage. And ultimately, I just needed something familiar. Just like how we crave nostalgic food when we're sick, I was craving for my car, even though it was a PT Loser.

A few days later as promised, I drove my car out of the shop and back home. I had saved all of my money for many months, forgoing all fun and activity for four things. First, I needed this car moved to Colorado. Done. Second, I needed this car working. Done. The third item on the list was this trip to the Badlands. After that, the fourth, it was the move back east. There were so many details and considerations for the move back east, but it could all wait. I needed this trip. I needed the beauty and the adventure.

Now that I had the car repaired and reliable with predictable gas mileage, I was able to plan the rest of the trip and all of the details. On the first day, I was going to do the drive to Rapid City in a single day, across the empty east side of Wyoming and quickly through the Black Hills. On the second day, I would go the Badlands and spend a day there. On the third day, I would begin the journey back to Colorado and spend a day in the Black Hills, seeing Mount Rushmore. On the fourth and final day, I'd drive back to Colorado. It was going to be a quick trip, nearly twelve-hundred miles from the driveway and back. I had a very tight budget, but it was workable and had a little flexibility. The plan was solid. I had reviewed it many times, making sure I knew the places to stop and see for fun, for gas, or for food. Wyoming is pretty empty, and it's easy to get caught between towns for hours. A lack of clarity and preparation could have been trouble for me, so I made sure I knew exactly where I was going and where I was going to stop along the way.

After what seemed like weeks of planning and preparing for such a short trip, the day finally came. I woke up before the sun and left the house while my mom, stepdad, and brothers were still asleep. I had said goodbye to them the night before and told them I'd be in touch as I could. I wasn't too sure of what kind of coverage my phone was going to have, so I made sure to clarify that I would reach out as I could. When I pulled out of the neighborhood before sunrise, I could feel the anxiety and anticipation of this trip building in me. It wasn't an anxiety that was built on worry, like much of the anxiety I had been carrying for the many months before this trip. It was an anxiety around excitement for what I was going to see and experience. I was anxious for new vision, new revelation, and new clarity as to where my life was supposed to go next. I literally had no direction in this season of my life. It was as if my prior life had completely ended, and I had memorialized it at the ranch. Now was the infancy of this new life filled with unknowns. What career would I have? Would I ever go back to a church? Would I ever have a family of my own? A house? Children? Would I ever find purpose for my life? A vision for my future? I believed many of these answers were somewhere along I-25 north or maybe somewhere on Highway 18 in Wyoming. And with that dream, I began heading north.

I made it around Colorado Springs before the morning commute, and as I headed toward Denver, the sunlight began to hit the peaks of the Rockies on my left. It was a very clear day, and the light from the east set the mountains ablaze. They were glowing orange and pink and purple, all the colors of sunrise. The tops of the mountains were lit like beacons, signal fires drawing me north. By the time the sun had come up, I had arrived in Denver. While I had planned the right time to leave Colorado Springs to avoid the morning commute, I hit Denver like a leaf in a rain gutter. I became one of the tens of thousands of cars clogging up and slowing down the daily progression of men and women to their jobs, careers, and purposes. It was a subtle reminder of what I was hoping to find during the next four days. While I was sitting in the Denver traffic, the sun finally came up and the official day had begun. I was facing an eight-hour drive that day. It could be done a little quicker, but I was especially excited to drive Highway 18 in Wyoming. It is one of the most secluded drives in the country, and I was looking forward to a very open road and a few small towns.

As I left the Denver metro and headed toward Cheyenne, I finally began to feel free to think. Parts of the drive were quiet, with the windows up and nothing on the radio. On other sections of the drive, I had the windows down and various 1970's music cranked up as loud as I could stand it. At any given time that day, I was somewhere in between those states in the car as I drove across Wyoming. And at all times, I was taking in the beauty of the prairies and processing all the questions I had been asking. I've mentioned my love for the beauty of nature many times, and I do absolutely love it. It affects the heart in a major way. There is only one thing that amplifies and exponentially increases the effect the beauty of nature has on me, and I believe on others too.

Solitude.

I don't mean loneliness, but solitude. It's both terrifying and exhilarating. While loneliness is a possible emotional response to solitude, solitude in and of itself is not a bad or harmful thing. Many people for thousands of years have used solitude to search themselves, search for God, and search for clarity. Jesus himself would withdraw from people, including his closest friends, to recharge his spirit in solitude. He did it to pray. He did it to take breaks from the crowds. Solitude is a worthy goal. And coupled with beauty, it can have a profound effect on us. I'm sure you've seen something beautiful before out in this world God has created, and you've seen it among a multitude of others. Some of the most beautifully documented places in the United States are also some of the most crowded. Try going to Yellowstone in the summer or the Grand Canyon's main overlooks. Even right here Shenandoah National Park, which is a relatively small park fairly close to my home, is crowded most days. It's increasingly difficult to go somewhere beautiful and not see other people.

Not Wyoming. I'll admit that not many would refer to an open prairie as beautiful, but to my eyes, it was something I've never seen. I loved every moment of that drive. And it was completely secluded. Total solitude. I could stop anywhere at anytime and just take it all in and not worry about anyone pulling up behind me or around me. Of course there came a little anxiety with that as well, as my phone was showing "no service" for almost the entire drive. If anything was to happen to my car again, I'd likely have to get creative to get some help. Every now and then on the drive, I'd come upon an incredibly long train snaking its way through the prairies along Highway 18. Maybe the conductor would see me and help me if my car broke down.

Not too far from the interstate on this lonely two-lane highway was a town called Lost Springs. As I was driving, I saw a state placed sign for Lost Springs with their name and census information. The sign said "Lost Springs, Population: 3." I did a double take, and it still said the same thing. We all have our definitions of small towns. People who are from larger cities usually equate a suburb with being a small town. Yet people not from the city would consider a suburb part of a greater metro area. People from the country live in small towns, but if you were to ever study a map of America, you'd see that many small towns are very close together. Lost Springs boasts that they were the smallest town in America, and it wasn't next door to any other town. Population of three? My mind was racing contemplating who these people were, living in this town. Were they related? Were they from Lost Springs, part of a line of generations who once settled here and had lives? Maybe there was something magical or special about the land that kept them there, much like the supposed vortexes of Sedona, Arizona. Maybe Lost Springs was one of the best kept secrets in America.

I pulled up to the left turn into Lost Springs from the highway. An old set of train tracks guarded the entrance to the city like a moat of a castle. You could see either direction for what seemed like miles, and there was no train on any horizon. I slowly drove over the tracks, my car bouncing at the rough state of the road and tracks, likely abused by winter after winter of snow and ice and no maintenance department of Lost Springs to maintain the quality of the roads. And just a few feet past the tracks, I entered the city limits of Lost Springs.

There were only a few buildings in the area, but it was obvious that at some point, more than three people lived here. On the left was an old block warehouse that had been abandoned for what seemed like decades ago. The windows were busted out, and many had been boarded up. Plants and birds were now occupying the space where someone once saw a vision through for a shop, or something industrial, or grain storage... I had no idea. Right across the street on my right were the general store and post office. The building had a classic look to it, like something you'd expect in the Wild West. No one really thinks of Wyoming as the Wild West. We think of the browns of Texas, Arizona, New Mexico, and train towns from the movies. Wyoming is a cowboy state. It was a "cowboys and Indians" state. It was the bison hunting state. "Hell on Wheels," the transcontinental railroad city of the Union Pacific came through this state and set up a home in Cheyenne. This general store looked like it belonged in that time. It was the classic Western look. The siding had been painted white decades earlier but today was faded and chipped. On the white siding, hand painted in all-cap red letters was the name "Lost Springs." Down the street past the general store was a town hall, with outhouses right outside. Directly across the street was the Lost Bar, which appeared to be still open and in use today. The rest of the immediate area was sprinkled with small buildings, a few campers and trailers that hunters seasonally used, and some sheds. That was all I saw. That was the entire city of Lost Springs.

But what caught my eye as I drove in was one of the residents. As I pulled into Lost Springs, there was an old man riding a lawn mower in the lot of the old warehouse. He saw me pull the car into town and stop in front of the general store. Immediately as if he hadn't seen an outsider for the many weeks, he waved, stopped the lawn mower, and came running over to me.

Every year of my life and for several generations before me, my father's family has gathered at the small church in Warsaw that I attended when I was young. My grandfather was one of eight children, and each of his siblings all went on to have their own families. My father grew up gathering at the family's church on every second Sunday in June for a family reunion, only a mile or so down the country road from where my grandfather was raised. By the time I was born, we were three to four generations still gathering at that church every second Sunday in June. I was a very special part of that day because I had actually been born on the second Sunday in June right on the annual gathering of the family. In some ways, I was a prodigy to the family. I was the "reunion baby." To this day the family still gathers every year, but now on the second Saturday in June, and I haven't really gone much in the last twenty years. My grandfather's generation is all but gone. My father's generation all left the Warsaw area. My generation came into adulthood during the birth of social media, so in some ways we have a reunion ongoing through our laptops and phones.

But I remember how I was embraced as a kid with so much excitement by my relatives every second Sunday in June when I was growing up. I hadn't seen that excitement for many years until I entered Lost Springs. Alfred Stringham quickly approached me, welcoming me to Lost Springs. He looked the part, too—older man with glasses from thirty years ago, with wild gray hair with a wild gray beard. His smile was warm and welcoming, in spite of his many aging and missing teeth. He wore what you'd expect a hearty older Wyoming man in the city of Lost Springs to wear: dusty jeans and an old button-up. After giving me a little information about the history of the city and answering a few of my questions, he led me into his general store. As we were walking in, I had asked him to tell me about life in this forgotten place. The other two residents were his brother, Art, and a woman named Leda Price. Alfred worked in the general store and post office, Leda worked in the bar, and I don't recall him telling me what his brother did. The three of them took turns being the mayor, and in this particular year, Alfred was fulfilling his civic duty. When he mentioned Leda and the bar, I asked him if it was just the three of them sitting there in the evenings having drinks. He told me that while that was normally the case, hunters often frequented the region and would rent the campers and trailers on the outskirts of town. After hunting, they'd come have drinks at the Lost Bar. I honestly found their whole lifestyle fascinating. I didn't ask, but I certainly wondered what kind of problems they'd have as a population of three. What was the town gossip and drama like? And what on earth did they spend their time doing, other than drinking at the bar.

When I came into the general store and post office, the place was full of antiques and various collectables, mostly leftovers from an earlier life of the city, as well as Alfred and his parents' collection from years of "junking." The cash register was nearly as old as the building, made of wood and iron. I looked around for a bit and then made a small purchase to support the local economy. On the counter was a small bowl of wooden coins that said "Lost Springs, Population: 3." Alfred handed me one to remember him and the town by. We said our goodbyes and I got back into my car. I made a U-turn in front of the store and headed back across the tracks and onto the highway. In my rearview mirror, I looked back as Lost Springs wandered off into the horizon. I had just met one of the residents in America's smallest town.

What's funny is that in our entire conversation, he never asked anything about me. Not that I wanted to volunteer anything to Alfred, but it was interesting that he was so used to being a roadside oddity that he didn't think to find out about the potentially lost traveler wandering upon Lost Springs. If I was in his shoes, I would basically trap anyone who came into the town and make them tell me all they could about life on the outside. I would want to hear about where they're from and definitely want to hear why they're on this secluded highway in this abandoned city. I'd need to hear about their adventures, where they've been, and where they're going. I'd invite them back and tell them to come visit again. But not Alfred. He wasn't interested in any of that. He didn't care where I was from or where I was going. He didn't concern himself with my affairs. He had a simple and quiet little life here, and he didn't preoccupy his thoughts with anything that was going to distract him from that. As soon as I left, I'm sure he went back to cutting the grass in front of the old warehouse.

To be Alfred. To not be concerned with the lives outside of your own. I looked Alfred up once on a few social media platforms. Nothing. I figured he'd at least have some connection to the outside world, but he doesn't or, at least, not that I could find. But even that inspires me. This guy is completely disconnected from what's going on outside of that small road and those small buildings. He didn't know what I was going through. He wasn't aware of how wrecked my life had been for the past year or how I was even that very day struggling to find vision for my life. He wasn't judging me or my failures. He was just happy to have someone to spend a few minutes with, and that was enough. I think too often we get so caught up worried about what others are thinking (or could be thinking) about us, like we're the center of their world. But the reality is, we're not. Most people, even people in our day-to-day lives, aren't concerning themselves with our lives. They've got their own grass to tend to, their own stores to run, and their own bars to enjoy themselves in. Just because we're the most important thing in our lives doesn't mean we're important at all to others. All of my failures, pain, and struggles of the past year weren't any concern to Alfred. And there was some freedom in that moment in Lost Springs.

THE BADLANDS

The flat prairies of Wyoming soon gave way to the slow rising Black Hills, like a ripple from the Rockies. This isn't a large region, less than half the size of Yellowstone. Yet it's full of iconic locations. There's the most famous place in the Black Hills, Mount Rushmore. There's also another carving in the mountain several miles south of Rushmore, Crazy Horse. Then there's Sylvan Lake, an iconic lake where movies like *National Treasure* had been filmed. There's Harney Peak (later renamed Black Elk Peak to honor the fallen Sioux people who were slaughtered by Harney), the highest elevation of the Black Hills, rising over seven-thousand feet. And one of the coolest things about the Black Hills is the free-roaming bison that are all over Custer State Park and the surrounding area. I had never seen a bison in the wild before until I came into the Black Hills. As I came around a bend, there was a large open field at the base of one of the mountain forests. That entire field was being grazed upon by a herd of bison. I pulled the car to the side of the road and just watched as these massive and mostly mythological creatures slowly moved around the field. As a guy from coastal North Carolina, I had only seen bison in pictures of the West, with cowboys and Indians. I hunted bison once while on the MS-DOS

Oregon Trail, but that had been my extent of experience with these beasts. I knew I'd see them on this trip, and I had heard not to approach them. Thankfully a quick search on YouTube for "bison attacks" would discourage anyone from getting too close. I watched from the window of my car as they went about their peaceful day, and then I continued with mine. I skipped the sights of the Black Hills and headed straight for Rapid City, where I planned to stay the night. The day had been incredibly long, as I had left Colorado early that morning. I had to drive home in a few days and planned to see the sights of the Black Hills on the way back. Right over the mountains was the largest city in the state, Rapid City.

I had been very excited to see this place. I actually had some nostalgia of Rapid City, even though I had never been there. About three years before this drive, I was living as a newlywed in the Shenandoah Valley of Virginia. I was working at a small church, and I was feeling a lot of internal conflicts. I was wrestling with my decision to get married when I did and to whom I married. I never want to make an excuse or shift blame for my poor decisions, but I had some influencers in my life during that season that I was not mature enough to handle. When you're a young man, in your university, learning about yourself as you come into adulthood, the last thing I'd recommend you have is a very serious girlfriend, fiancé, or wife. I ended up with all three during my time in school. As a freshman, I got a serious girlfriend. In my sophomore year, I got a fiancé. Right before my senior year, she became my wife. And at twenty-two years old, I entered into a marriage, a covenant intended to be so serious and committed. I wouldn't have given myself a two-hundred-dollar loan then. What in the world made me think I was mature enough to get married? I watched this progression over and over at the small, Christian university I went to.

Paul says in 1 Corinthians 7:9 that "it's better for a man to marry than to burn with passion." You know what's even better than that? Self-control, patience, and rational and timely decisions about major and life-altering actions. I'm certainly not disagreeing with what Paul says here, but I think there's a third option, and I wish I would have taken it.

But I didn't. And I was miserable living in Virginia. I was working at her home church, where her father was one of my bosses. I wasn't close with my family, yet I was constantly forced upon hers. They are great people and a great family. That level of family involvement just wasn't for me, though. I wasn't used to lunch every Sunday at grandma's house or random weeknights with the parents. I needed my space and needed it fast. I had quietly begun looking for another job and looking as far away from Virginia as possible. Rapid City seemed to fit the bill. In my search, I came upon a job posting for a church in South Dakota in this town I had never heard of. I sent my resume and information and within twenty-four hours received a call from one of the church leaders. We spoke for an hour that day as I paced around the back lot of the church I was planning to leave. It initially seemed like a good fit. It seemed like a great job and church. It paid much better than I was making in Virginia, and it was about as far from her family as I could be. For the next several weeks, the church leaders and I got to know each other on the phone, and I studied all about Rapid City. I learned about the housing market, the grocery stores, and the day-to-day life. I learned about the surrounding nature and what kind of places would be easily accessible for when I needed to recharge. I studied the weather and familiarized myself with their short summers and harsh winters. I learned the roads and geography. There wasn't much about Rapid City I didn't find out over these weeks. But at the end of it all, it wasn't meant to be, and the conversations trickled off.

Here I was, finally able to see this place. I was going to drive the familiar streets and maybe picture the life I could have had. As I drove into town, I was taken back by how small Rapid City actually was. Since learning about Rapid City, I had moved to Charlotte, North Carolina, and then out to Colorado Springs. Rapid City was the size of one of their suburbs, at best. I quickly found the church I had been talking to those many years ago, and it was a lot smaller than I imagined it was too. I tried to picture what life would have been like as I drove up and down the streets of this small town. I imagined who I'd become here. This town seemed small enough to know everyone. I'd see a group of young adults walking downtown and wonder if I would have had community with them. What would we have done for fun? All of these thoughts were racing through me as the nostalgia for this place I'd never been was sweeping over me like an incoming tide.

Yet that's not how things went. And we cannot play the "what if" game. It is a dead-end road. What happened, happened. And what happens, happens. Our ability to make peace with our present and our past has a direct effect on the projection of our future. If we cannot come to terms with where we are and what got us here, how can we ever control where we're going? We don't always get to control our situations; in fact I'd say many more things happen to us than we give credit to. Not everything is your fault. Some things just happen. But you can completely control how you respond. Maybe not right away, but you can control yourself. Making peace with your present and past is within your control. You are fully capable of resolving anything if you want to. What's hard is that the easiest thing to do is the most painful thing, and that is to not deal with it. I had learned at the ranch to come to terms with the journey I had traveled and accept it. I accepted where I had been and where I was today. And in doing so, I had freedom to decide for myself what my future would look like. I was fully in control of this moment.

That night, I stayed at a historic hotel in downtown Rapid City. It was actually the cheapest hotel in the area and by the pictures looked like an incredible place. Opened in 1928, this hotel had been around for a long time. It still had much of the original woodworking and design as it did when it first opened. When I walked in, I immediately thought I had stepped into the half-sister hotel from *The Shining.* Even the lobby made me uncomfortable. When I checked into my room, I was significantly freaked out by this place. It was mostly vacant. It felt eerie. It was poorly lit. It creaked. It had dark colors and old wallpaper. I'm pretty sure there was mold in the windowsill and bathroom. I'm also pretty sure there was blood on the ceiling, which was a mystery in and of itself. It smelled like someone was smoking next door, though no one else was even on my hall. I honestly don't remember if I even slept much that night. Recently in Los Angeles, I met someone from Rapid City named Ashley. I told her about my first experience in the town and staying in that creepy hotel. She told me that every local knows it's haunted. While I don't necessarily believe in ghosts, I do believe something is up with that hotel, and I don't plan on returning. I couldn't have checked out fast enough that morning. Rapid City ended up not being for me after all.

That morning it was onto the climax of this road trip, the Badlands. About an hour east of Rapid City among the largest undisturbed grassland in America is a geological anomaly of buttes and pinnacles of earth and rock that create a prehistoric-looking landscape for miles and miles. You enter it mostly from the flattops as you drive in, and you can see massive valleys and canyons formed by millennia of erosion and wind. What's even more interesting is to see the stripes and colors among the canyons, every layer representing a year, decade, millennium, or eon, or eons as old as the earth itself. This is the kind of landscape you'd expect to look across and see a herd of dinosaurs moving through. It looks like the land before time. Off in the distance south of the Badlands is a grass sea with a dormant navy of bison to the horizon. While one of America's National Parks, the Badlands is not easily accessible. The only city with an airport that connects to the rest of the nation's airports is Rapid City, and it's essentially a small regional airport. Other than Rapid City, there is no way to get to the Badlands without driving nearly double-digit hours. Omaha, Minneapolis, and Denver are the closest big cities, the closest being Denver, which I had driven through the day before.

When I entered the Badlands, I chose my route and began to drive through the park. I stopped at several places to look around, and walk a bit. I was alone in this vastly quiet, empty, and dead place. There is an ecosystem here, but it's pretty hidden. Very few plants are growing in the Badlands, and the mice and prairie dogs aren't exactly making their presence known to you as you wonder around. On this day, it was just me and the earth beneath my feet. Years later I would return to this very spot and camp here on the night of a new moon. Since the night was void of any light pollution, the heavens were lit from the horizon to the horizon. Never before or since have I seen a sky so vast and full. There was a star in every pixel of the sky. Truly there is nothing out here in the Badlands.

The Lakota people first named the Badlands "mako sica," literally meaning "land bad." Later French-Canadian fur trappers would refer to the land as "les mauvais terres pour traverse," or "bad lands to travel through." And it is, even today. The roads wind around and through the canyons without logic or reason in a series of flat runs and switchbacks. If you had to navigate through this place on foot, I'm sure you'd face a lot of frustrations and even danger. People haven't lived here. People haven't farmed here. This is just bad land. Yet it's beautiful. It's otherworldly. It's a singular anomaly in this country and even the world. What it seemingly lacks in worth it makes up for in wonder. And that makes it invaluable.

For me there was a great lesson in this. Singer-songwriter Derek Webb has a song where he says we're "all crooked deep down," and maybe that's true. In the church, a major sect of Christianity who follows a four-hundred-year-old theologian named John Calvin says all of mankind if totally deprived, incapable of doing any good on their own. The NIV Bible, which is arguably the most widely distributed modern Bible translation, intentionally misinterprets the Greek word *sarx*, which literally means "flesh," as the phrase "sinful nature" so that you believe by design your nature is sinful, incapable of good. And while I personally disagree, maybe all of these are doctrinally correct. No one can tell you for certain on this side of heaven because this very topic in Christendom has been debated for hundreds of years. Regardless, maybe this is where we are as a creation: crooked, deprived, and sinful by nature.

Badlands. Maybe we are Badlands, our total being eroded by the storms of life, slowly trimmed by the winds of force and change. Maybe we're prehistoric, with nothing but buried bones within our "sarx," void of life, where the only life within us remains hidden and refuses to show itself because it's afraid of what authenticity and transparency may yield. Judgment and anxiety and fear and worry, all like thorns and thistles making the land incapable of producing anything good or beneficial. When others see us, they see our flaws and failures and say under their breath, "mako sica." They don't walk through life with us, and instead choose to say "les mauvais terres pour traverse."

And you know what, maybe they're exactly right. I knew what it felt like to be eroded by the storms of divorce, loss, betrayal, embarrassment, and failure. I knew how damaging the winds of change could be and have felt those winds blow against me many times, especially in the year leading up to this moment. I felt prehistoric. I felt like Jesus said of the Pharisees, as a "whitewashed tomb full of dead man's bones." The life in me is so easily replaced by fear and worry. My career had been covered with thorns and thistles. And I knew what it felt like to be pointed at and accused, even by close friends.

But as I looked into the Badlands, what had started in me at the ranch like wet concrete poured into a new mold had finally hardened. I was Badlands, *and that was ok.* Because unlike these Badlands that have laid unchanged and unproductive for eons, I am capable of controlling my future. I had made peace with my past and my present. Alfred didn't care about my failures or my story, and in that brief moment in Lost Springs, I learned that my company can be something people can get excited about and that they didn't need to know my journey to value me, my friendship, or my time. They would just value me because I showed up. I am Badlands, *and that's ok.* What was once my present in this moment in South Dakota is now part of my collective past, and it's full of wonder. It brought me to where I am today.

As I studied the map to prepare for the drive home, I decided to take a detour. I had done a little better with mileage than I thought I was going to and was fairly ahead on my budget. Rather than return the way I came, I'd go a little further west. I left the Badlands, stopped at the famous roadside attraction Wall Drug Store, and then headed back into the Black Hills. I went to Mount Rushmore and saw the presidents.

I then swung northwest toward another curious geological anomaly in America called Devil's Tower. I saw the monument to the six girls who were picking flowers when a giant grizzly bear attacked them. Thankfully they were saved by the Great Spirit, who raised the earth beneath their feet to protect them. The bear attempted to climb the pillar, grinding away at the stone and leaving deep jagged scratches in the rock. The girls were safe up top in the wildflower field. Or so the legend says. Then I headed south back to Colorado Springs for what was next.

THE NORTH

When I left for the Badlands, I had a goal for myself. It was to get clarity and vision for what was next. The hours upon hours in the car in the wilderness gave me plenty of time to think through this and work through scenarios in my head. I had determined a few things for certain. First, I was going to leave the job at the little cafe and leave Colorado. I was going to go back to the east coast for a little while. While there, I was going to put some feelers out there to see if there was a church that would want me to work for them. I had spent nearly a year of my life feeling like I was worthless to God and to any church, but God was restoring my purpose. I was dreaming again of what a healthy ministry could be. I was dreaming of health for myself and what kind of church I'd want to help build.

I've never been very evangelical. Maybe that's a core problem with my faith. I've always seen myself as someone who tends to the sheep rather than someone who goes and finds lost sheep. It's not that I don't care about the lost sheep. I really do care. But I have an internal philosophy that, up to this point in my life, I was unable to live out and work through. I've always felt it was irresponsible to share my faith with someone if I wasn't going to walk with them. I felt this responsibility, maybe unrealistically, that if I told them about my faith and they took it as their own, I was responsible for nurturing that faith within them. As I think on this season of my faith and maturity, I think I was very well-intentioned but also very arrogant about my role in another person's faith. I don't mean arrogant in a conceded, cocky, and irrationally self-assured way, but arrogant in making too much of myself and my role in their faith no room for the Holy Spirit.

When I was in college, I played guitar and sang in a regionally successful band. We were a unique setup and had a really entertaining show. In a time where hip-hop music was mostly driven by producers with computers, we did hip-hop with a live band. Our grooves and riffs were inspired by rock, pop, and jazz, and our emcee would rap over the live band. It had *crazy* energy. We were so committed to this band and one another that we would rehearse every Tuesday and Thursday at six in the morning before our classes. I'd be rolling my amp across the parking lot of the dorm to our chapel (where we rehearsed) in the dark nearly the entire school year. And that dedication paid off. We played some great venues and shows and had an incredible experience together. Those are some of my favorite memories of playing music. The five of us had something special.

It was also the height of Myspace, and we had a pretty robust Myspace presence. We also had a solid Myspace strategy, which I oversaw. I'd go to zip codes we were going to play a show and add people as friends. I did this from my personal page rather than the band page, and then I'd post recent updates and links to the band's page. I'd look at our calendar and for several months and I'd blow up an area with our information. I also did this in towns we were personally connected too. I was working at a small church in the western part of Virginia, so I hit up that area. Nick, our emcee, was living and working in Williamsburg,

Virginia, so I hit up Williamsburg. We all had connected our lives in college in Elizabeth City, North Carolina, so I hit up that place too. If we had any presence, I'd add friends on Myspace.

It wasn't unusual for someone to comment or message me in response. Most people accepted the request and then went on with their lives. But there was a decent amount of people who would check out my page, the band's page, and listen to our music. They were exactly who I was after. I loved reading their comments or getting their messages. It affirmed that the plan was working. I logged into Myspace once and had a message from a girl in my area named Justine. I had added her and hundreds of others sometime during that week, and she wrote me and asked who I was and why I added her. Before I saw that first message to respond, she had looked at my Myspace page and saw I was the youth and music leader for a local church. She then sent a message asking about the church. I responded to her messages and learned about her family. It was her and her husband Zach and their toddler son Christopher. That Sunday, the three of them came to our church, and we all immediately connected. They had no church background. They were a spiritual blank slate, which is a rarity in the south. We became friends with them, and they later went on a ski trip with us and our youth group to help supervise the teenagers. While on that trip, I sat down with them and shared the Gospel. They both responded, and that weekend when we got home, they were baptized. They became an integral part of my ministry there. They were a major part of my life in that season.

But not long after, I moved to Charlotte. I left them there, at a small and dying church. I watched from afar as they continued to carry what I had built, but things were slipping away. I watched from afar as Zach's younger brother Austin, who had moved in with them, got into some serious trouble and they didn't know how to walk through it. Then I watched from afar as Justine and Zach split up. While I was in Colorado after my divorce, I got an email from my ex that I needed to call the hospital in western Virginia, because at the end of his rope, Zach had shot himself in the head and had miraculously survived and was on life support. I kept close tabs to the situation as best as I could from Colorado, and when Zach had regained his ability to speak, I called him at the hospital. It had been a long time since we spoke, but I told him I was sorry and that I loved him and that I was there for him through anything.

But all the while, I felt so guilty. I should have stayed there in Virginia. Zach and Justine were spiritually my responsibility. If I would have been there, I could have helped through the situation with his brother. Honestly, the situation involved a leader who replaced me that ended up causing physical and emotional harm for Austin, and I really struggled with the fact that if I would have never left, he would have never taken that job, and maybe this entire chain of events wouldn't have unfolded. If I had been there, when the hard times hit Zach and Justine, I could have met with them, counseled them, and helped them. And if I would have been there, maybe Zach would have reached out to me when he lost all hope and put the gun barrel to his head.

This is why I'm not evangelical. I'd rather tend to sheep than lead someone somewhere I may not be. For my entire life, I've personally deeply struggled with the feeling of abandonment. Yet I was for sure going to abandon people. I wouldn't do it maliciously or intentionally, but as someone who has always been unsettled and nomadic, I cannot guarantee anyone in any geographical location that I will still be there a year from now. I had abandoned Zach and Justine, but there was more on that list, more stories of situations that maybe I could have prevented or helped walk through.

What happened, happened. And what happens, happens. Maybe in all of the happening, I could find a way to be evangelical after all. Even looking at the New Testament, Paul himself moved around from place to place sharing the Gospel and then handing the growth process off to the local church. Maybe there was some precedence for me to feel free to do the same. After all, someone who is in the church but refuses to be evangelical is a fraud. And I was tired of being a fraud. I had owned my faith, or at least was owning it. I was nurturing it and healing it. The god who abandoned me in Arkansas was no longer my god, and I had found the true God, who never leaves us or forsakes us. The version of God I had known for so many years never really was who I thought He was, and I had found this new Father who actually loved me unconditionally, in all of my greatness and all of my weakness. He loved me in my struggles and dark days just as much as he loved the days where I won. That's a God worth sharing about. And I wanted to give my life to helping others meet this God or know this God better than they did. Free people free people, and I wanted to make it my life mission to free people.

But first, I had to tie up some loose ends. Life in Colorado wasn't sustainable. Everyday as I worked that job at the cafe, I felt a growing lack of purpose. I figured out exactly what I needed to save to get back east, made arrangements with a distant relative who had plenty of space for me to stay for a few weeks, and then hit the road. I drove from Colorado to North Carolina as quickly as I could. On the first day, I made it seventeen hours. I slept for a few hours at a roadside motel and then drove ten hours the next day. I made it to Wilmington, North Carolina, and crashed for a few days.

I had come to North Carolina for three reasons. First was to pick up all of my remaining belongings from Charlotte. I had left for Colorado fairly quickly and desperately earlier that year, and a friend of mine had stored the few things I had left in the spare bedroom of his house. I very much appreciated him doing that for me, but some things had unfolded while I was in Colorado. I don't know if it was distance, lack of communication, or division being sown between my friends and I from the situation I was in, but he needed me to get my belongings out of his house. I told him I'd come within the month, and I meant to keep my word.

The second reason I came to North Carolina was to rest physically, mentally, and emotionally. I didn't know anyone outside of my distant relatives in Wilmington, and other than helping me out with a place to stay for a while, I really had no interaction with them. I needed time for myself to think, pray, meditate, and make some decisions. I had been talking to a church up north, in a very small community just west of Minneapolis. I had never been up north to Minnesota before, but I was really enjoying getting to know their leadership. Maybe this was what was next. But to know for sure, I needed time to get to know them and to see if that was where God was calling me. It's hard to hear His voice calling if I'm surrounded by distractions, and there wouldn't be any distractions here in Wilmington.

The third and final reason I came back to North Carolina was to record new music I had written throughout the separation and divorce. Writing has always been therapeutic for me. In college I loved writing papers. I also loved journaling and blogging. When I had confidence in myself artistically, I began writing songs. My first collection of songs was written in an internal descent while I was still married. I wrote about impending change and all of the feelings associated with it. While it sounds like fairly dark content, the album itself was very upbeat and positive, almost making light of the darker lyrics and content. It was kind of like my life in that season: feeling hopeless while masking it with happiness and joy. "Look to the East" was my first project, and it was time for the follow-up. And this new project, written throughout the divorce, was much more honest and actually *sounded* like the lyrics felt. The penultimate song on that album was a song I wrote to my ex as an apology and hopefulness that one day I would fall in love again and do it better:

"I knew this day was coming, I knew it all so well
I thought I could prevent it, but you cannot prevent hell
I didn't do my best, I didn't play my hand
Now I hope I get another shot to be a better man
I said I wouldn't fight you anymore about the truth
Its burdens on the winner, and you know I would lose
I've tried and tried to tell you, but you could not understand
Now I hope I get another shot to be a better man
I promise that the next time I'll give it all I've got
And while that doesn't mean too much to you,
to me it means alot
I guess that's what I'm saying, I guess that's what I've planned
I just hope I get another shot to be a better man
A new season is coming where everything will start to change
And friends will become awkward,
and things will become strange
I promise not to tell them
that we were doomed where we began
I just hope I get another shot to be a better man
When everything is finished and the dust all settles down

I'll write you a letter from my new state and town
I'm sorry for the hurt, I guess that is my special brand
I just hope I get another shot to be a better man."

There was a small studio in Wilmington that I wanted to record in, and I offered to barter with them on something they needed: a new website. They were still running a GeoCities website that was at least a decade old, and the web was ever evolving. I had experience building my bands and music websites over the years, so on a whim I contacted the owner of the studio, told him what I needed, and offered to build him a new website for it. Much to my surprise, he loved the idea, and I had my studio time booked. I recorded "The Perfect Candidate" in only a few days, tracking every instrument myself. And I got their website up and running, so the situation worked great.

Life in North Carolina was actually a lot more difficult than I had anticipated. I only had a limited amount of money to survive on and no end in sight. I looked around for a job, even something part-time, but the recession had hit North Carolina hard, and there was nothing to be had. Like most places, you need connections, and even though I know Wilmington very well, I didn't know anyone there. One thing I really didn't consider when coming back east was that I'd have to eat on my own. At my mother's house in Colorado, I may have had stress but I at least had food. Here in Wilmington, I had to get my own food, and as I quickly found out, food is expensive. It was too expensive to eat out and too expensive to buy groceries. Plus, things were going really well with the church in Minnesota, and at any time they could invite me up. I didn't want to settle too deeply into North Carolina, even too deeply into the refrigerator. But time kept moving on, and money kept running out. I began selling off various music equipment I had. I had some old touring equipment from the hip-hop days, and one item at a time ended up at the pawnshop. By the time the church in Minnesota flew me up to visit for a weekend, I was only eating jasmine rice in a rice cooker with salt and pepper, and I'd mix in a cup of noodles with it if I was feeling fancy. I skipped breakfast everyday and ate a large bowl of rice for lunch and a smaller bowl for dinner. It was a very stressful season, but compared to the stress I was feeling earlier that year, this was nothing. There are different kinds of stress, and while no stress is enjoyable, this was tolerable.

I was really skeptical about Minnesota. It wasn't the church or the people or the situation at all. I had a lot of doubt in my ability to live up there. It was the late fall, and I was daily keeping an eye on the north. I had lived in a colder climate before, but nothing like I was seeing in Minnesota. It wasn't even just the cold weather, it was all of the snow. I was looking at the *Farmers' Almanac* and annual climate reports, doing my research on how anyone can live in a place where the average low in the wintertime is single digitals, and for much of January, the temperature is below zero, with thirty to seventy inches of snow in any given year. Even when I lived in Germany for three years, our coldest days maybe got into the teens, and the most snow I ever remember having was in my senior year of high school when we got nearly a foot of snow one winter. Otherwise, being from North Carolina, snow is something you only see every few years and maybe only an inch or two. Temperatures rarely get much below the mid-twenties. Minnesota would be a big change.

When I landed in Minneapolis, it was cold and raining. Seeing the Twin Cities from the sky as I approached the airport was like looking into a snow globe. At some point, snow had already covered the ground, yet the weather wasn't quite cold enough for all precipitation to be snow just yet. The light drizzle in the cold air wasn't an encouraging sign. Two guys came to pick me up that day, Billy and David. Billy was from Oregon but had spent his entire career in the Midwest.

David was local to the area, a true Minnesotan. They seemed excited to see me there. And honestly, I was excited to be there. I hadn't stepped into a church or been around any church people in many months since I left the church in Colorado. Though I had been nurturing my faith as best I knew how in that season, I was doing it as an orphan. It was good to be back around people that would help nurture me as well. Billy and David took me to get some food and then showed me around the Twin Cities for a little bit. They spoke of great restaurants, cool guitar shops, and odd places I'd need to see. We were able to do a few things that day, like eat pizza at Cossetta's in Saint Paul and stop off at Willie's American Guitars. They drove me by the Mall of America in Minneapolis, and then we continued over to Highway 12 to head west toward the small town of Dassel. The road to Dassel is a small town after small town, every five miles or so, for an hour. All of these little towns have people that farm, work in various industries or factories, or commute to the cities. Wayzatta, Maple Plain, Delano, Montrose, Waverly, Howard Lake, Cokato, and, finally, Dassel.

When we pulled into the town, I realized how small it really was. The population of Dassel was barely over a thousand people, with a small local grocery store, a service station or two, a diner and a bar, and a coffee shop. The church was on the main road as soon as you came into town, and within eyesight you could see two other churches. There were a total of five very different churches in the city. If you continued on the main road, you came to an intersection where Highway 12 meets Highway 15, and that marked the end of Dassel. There are many neighborhoods in suburbs of large and even medium-sized cities that are larger than the entire town of Dassel.

We turned off the main road and into the church parking lot. The church was exactly how I expected it. It was a typical brick building, with two floors. You'd enter into the stairwell, and you could go up to the lobby, offices, and auditorium or downstairs to a fellowship hall and a couple of classrooms for children. It wasn't a large church by any means, but the auditorium could easily seat around a hundred and fifty people or so, wall to wall. The church had been struggling to grow for years, and Billy had moved there and brought a lot of life and energy to the church. He was young, outspoken, and bold. That resonated well with this community, which was used to old men behind a pulpit preaching sermons they had written in seminary in the nineteen sixties. Billy was at about half the age of the other four Lead Pastors in town. He was definitely the only one that wasn't fully gray. And Billy didn't care too much about my story. I was transparent with him about where I had been. He knew about my divorce and all I had spent that last year struggling with. He knew my apprehension toward going back into ministry but that I had been called to it and knew it was my purpose. He knew that I was healing and needed a place that would help me in that process.

I met the church elders that evening. These were the men chosen by the congregation to lead the church's business. There was Randy, the local butcher. He was quiet and stern. His wife and five children all worked in the butcher shop together, slaughtering and butchering cattle and goats every day. There was Dan, a local engineer. Dan was warm, and you could feel his kindness just from being in the same room as him. Dan had two sons who were finishing school. Galen was the local farmer, farming ten thousand acres with his two brothers and family. And then there was Tom, the lead elder, though I don't think he saw himself that way. Tom was inquisitive and full of wisdom. These men made up the elders of the church, and they were with whom full authority rested. Any staff reported to them, and they made the final decisions regarding any of the church's operation.

That evening, we got to know one another a little deeper. I had conversed with each of them on the phone at some point, but it was great to sit in the same room with them and dream a little about what that church could be. I heard the needs they had, and they heard the needs I had. We spent several hours that evening together, and then we went our separate ways. Billy took me to a local hotel in the next town over, and I settled in for the evening. Sunday came, and I led the band and music for the church. The job I was interviewing for was for music and creative arts, so I needed to demonstrate to them that I had that skill set. I gave them my best that weekend, and they received it well. The church really seemed to take to me. It was only eighty or ninety people, but it was enough to comfortably support the operation of the church. And they supported me. The church and I really clicked together. By the time I left that afternoon, I had fallen in love with this place. It was everything I wasn't and represented everything I never thought I would be. What better place to rebuild my life than somewhere like this. Now, I had to get the job offer.

I returned back to North Carolina and to my rice stockpiles. When I left the church before flying home, they gave me a thank you card for being there that weekend and had written me a check for my role on Sunday. This was completely unexpected, and their generosity toward me is the only reason I survived the next several weeks back in North Carolina. Even before they committed to me, they were caring for me. This was the kind of community I needed and so desperately desired. A few days into being back and I got a call from Billy. He said they loved me and wanted to offer me the job. I accepted, and just a few weeks later, I was headed north.

MINNESOTA

Billy had flown to North Carolina right after Thanksgiving to meet up with me. I had a small U-Haul with my limited furniture and possessions, basically what I had kept from my prior life. I also had my car. My original plan was to drive the U-Haul and pull the car behind me, but Billy wanted to make the drive with me. He would drive the truck, and I would drive the car. We would caravan across the United States toward Dassel. I had come to visit my father and his family before heading north, and Billy met us at his house. He flew in early in the morning, and we got on the road the same day. It was going to be a two very full days of driving to Minnesota from North Carolina, over ten hours a day. We made a few stops to entertain ourselves along the way as well and took breaks to eat together. I had done many long road trips throughout the last year, so I wasn't afraid of the time or the distance. I was more anxious about the new life I was about to begin. North Carolina to Virginia, Virginia to West Virginia, West Virginia to Kentucky, Kentucky to Indiana, and then Illinois, Wisconsin, and, finally, Minnesota. The Twin Cities appeared on the horizon as the sun was setting behind them from my view on I-94. This was it. This was my new home.

I knew as I crossed the state line that this wouldn't be forever. I had no idea how long it was going to be, but in my gut I knew this was temporary. I was feeling a sense of peace while all the while I felt a rush of restlessness rising within me. When I was growing up in eastern North Carolina, we spent many years in Wilmington. This was my mother's hometown. When my parents divorced when I was ten, we moved there full-time. While living there, my brother and I surfed a lot at Carolina Beach. I remember days where it would be fairly sunny and still above our heads while we were out surfing, but out at sea there would be a dark cloud on the horizon. Slowly the ocean would rise and swell as whatever was going on out there on the horizon came crawling toward the shore. Those days were some of our best surfing because the turbulence offshore would make the waves a little bigger, a little faster, a little more risky, and a lot more exciting. This was my feeling as I passed through Minneapolis on my way to the small church in the tiny town of Dassel. I knew this is where I was supposed to be. I was in the line up to catch the incoming wave. But like a wave, it was eventually going to crumble and fade into the shore.

I think that so much of life is like this. Nothing is really definite or even predictable. Even today something could change the course of my life. Sometimes the wave comes in through an email or phone call with an offer or opportunity we weren't planning on but can't pass up. Sometimes the wave is tragic, and we get crushed by hundreds and thousands of gallons of water that push us under and toss us around like we're weightless. Whether good or bad is really relative. Oftentimes the outcome of surfing is on the skill and will of the surfer. I've seen guys out at Virginia Beach on an incredibly tiny day riding wave after a wave having a blast, while I can't catch anything. Some of that is that I'm too fat or slow to maneuver myself into the right place and position. In fact, all of it is that I'm too fat and slow. And it's on me.

Yes, there are days where no one is enjoying themselves. Right before

Hurricane Florence hit the east coast, my brother and I paddled out with a friend who had never surfed before. We shouldn't have been out there. It was so choppy and rough, with the rain pouring down. But the waves were big, and we were determined to get something out of it. Our friend struggled for about five minutes, couldn't get past the breakers, and gave up. We saw him lying on the sand, with hands on his chest trying to catch his breath. I made it maybe fifteen minutes and zero rides before I finally gave up. I felt like I had been sprinting the entire time. My brother Daniel caught one wave and got slammed. He came in soon after me. Sometimes, there is no reason to be out there. We're not where we should be, and no amount of skill or will is going to help that.

I had made the decision to move a thousand miles away from my nearest family, friend, or relative. I had chosen to move to the coldest and snowiest state in the continental US. I had chosen a slower-paced life in a small town. I had chosen the seven-hundred-square-foot rental house with a refrigerator that was barely larger than the one I had in my college dorm room. I had chosen to work with Billy. I had chosen to live and work among farmers, factory workers, and close-knit families where I was an outsider. All of these things were mine and mine alone. This was going to be my life, by my decision. And I was happy with my decision. I was afraid. I knew it wasn't going to be forever. But I also knew I needed this. I needed this place and this pace. I needed a season of restoration, whether it would take a single year or several years.

It was dark when we pulled up to the house. One of the locals named Jesse was there, and he helped Billy and I unload the truck. It wasn't much, really. After all, the house was only seven-hundred-square feet, so it didn't take much time to unload it all and set it up. Then Billy and Jesse left, and I was alone for the first night in my new place. I didn't even have a mattress or bed. I didn't have blankets or sheets. I unrolled my old sleeping bag that I had bought for some camping trips when I was younger and crawled in. Night one. But by the end of the first month, I had upgraded the floor and a sleeping bag to a used futon and a sleeping bag. It was also winter, and winter had come in strong. Minnesota was white from border to border with over a foot of snow. It was colder than anywhere I had ever been in my life. I was sleeping in a hoodie every night, with the hood over my head. I couldn't get warm at all that first winter. I stayed in a state of shiver. I was also having a bit of trouble finding my place at the church and in the community. It's pretty amazing how different parts of the country can have such different cultures. I was from the southeast, where everyone assumed you were good and decent until you proved them wrong. This is especially true in the church. There is an honor and affirmation given to church staff from day one.

This was not the case at the church in Dassel. I was an obvious outsider to this community. Everyone was friendly to me, but everyone was skeptical of me. There was no positional honor or affirmation given. I was just another guy at the church. I never felt I started off with them at a deficit, but I definitely started at zero. I could either gain ground through loving them, being authentic, and being consistent, or like many other staff before me, I could lose their respect and trust. This church had a long history of quick turnovers in their staff. Now that I've been a worker in the church world for some time, I can attest that I've seen the high turnovers in ministry time after time. It is especially true in small churches in small towns. Even during my time in Minnesota, I watched churches in our community go through pastor after pastor or church staff after church staff. I was one of the veterans for a season, and I honestly wasn't there too long myself. So of course, I understood and even today still understand the skepticism to trust me in my first year at the church in Dassel. But I invested. I spent time getting to know people in their homes and in their worlds. I truly cared for their families and valued their friendships. In return, I received the same thing. And before too long, I had become one of them.

Several years ago I was watching a biopic about Jay Moriarity, a surfer from Santa Cruz who famously surfed Mavericks in California. The movie *Chasing Mavericks* was about his childhood and adolescence learning to surf from his mentor Frosty Hesson. There is a line in that movie that has always really resonated with me. In the scene, Frosty is struggling to accept the role he was playing in Jay's life. Jay had been abandoned by his father, and it's obvious in the film that he looked at Frosty like a father though Frosty didn't acknowledge it himself. In a powerful moment in the movie, Frosty's wife Brenda says to him:

"There are all kinds of sons. Some are born to you, some just occur to you."

I may not have known it then, but I can say with confidence now that the elders of the church in Dassel had a huge impact on shaping my life. I don't know if they would ever say they collectively saw me as a son, but I can tell you that I saw myself as a son to them. In fact, I credit them to who I am today more than I credit anyone in my life. They each personally invested something in me, and perhaps one day I'll write about the impact these four men had on my life.

North. The north is where my life got a reset: new people, new territory, new networks and new friends. New restaurants and places to explore, and a new love.

I had met Amanda a few years before. Once things didn't work out in Rapid City, I was trying to find anything I could to get me out of Virginia. I had taken a job in Charlotte, and my former wife and I had relocated in the summer from the Shenandoah Valley to the Queen City. It was only a few months later that I met Amanda for the first time. I've always had a very photographic memory, and I can still remember the day I first saw Amanda. I remember where I was standing and what she was wearing. I was in the balcony of the converted traditional church I was working at. What was once full of pews was now a production center and an office. I was behind the sound board with our front of house engineer, and I saw Amanda walk across the room. She piqued my curiosity because I had met just about every young adult in that church over the last few months. In fact, my former wife and I had started a weekly social gathering of all the young people at our church. It was mostly a middle-aged or older congregation, so anyone in that eighteen to twenty-five age bracket really stood out. Though as quick as Amanda appeared, she disappeared. It would be several more months before I'd see her again.

Months later, she returned. She had grown up in this church, and had decided to come back this particular Sunday with her parents who attended every week. It was that week that a member of the church sought me out to introduce Amanda to me so that I could invite her to our group of young adults. We introduced ourselves to each other, and I gave her our information. The next evening, Amanda came to our group gathering. The thing that surprised me about Amanda that evening was that she came to our house drunk. She had been drinking with a friend and decided at the last minute to attend our group. I'm not sure if the other twenty people in the room noticed or would have said anything if they had noticed. We were a place for anyone and everyone. That night as Amanda sobered up, she met our friend circle and began assimilating into our lives.

The next couple of years, Amanda completely changed her life. It's really her story to tell, and perhaps one day she will share how she left a life of drugs, alcohol, abuse, and emptiness all for what Jesus says is a "life to the fullest." She is a testimony that people who want their lives to change can change their lives. I believe in absolutes, but I also believe a lot of things in life are relative. Struggles with addictions are not life sentences. They can be overcome.

Three years after I met Amanda, her life looked completely different than it did the first time she came to our group. Since moving to Colorado, Amanda and I became pen pals through our phones. We would talk almost every day. She was the only connection to my prior life, and what began as situational updates became conversations about life, loss, and ultimately the future. We were both fairly alone at this time, but we had companionship with one another even though we were fifteen-hundred miles apart. It was actually a blessing to build something in distance and different time zones. The only thing we had for that entire first year was great conversation.

Since I had moved up to Minnesota, Amanda and I had started talking about what officially dating could look like and what it would take for her to move from Charlotte to Minnesota. We weren't sure how it would be perceived from friends we shared, especially friends from our past who knew my life before. In some ways I was afraid that I would be chained up again to the past I had worked so hard to break free from. Would all of the work I did on myself in Colorado and at the ranch and all of the healing I had experienced over the last year be jeopardized by starting a new relationship in Minnesota? Also, I had failed at marriage already. Though I was young and hopeful to have a long life ahead of me, could I even get married again, especially in the church world? It's one thing to get divorced and still be in ministry. It's another to remarry. There are some sects and denominations that would have anyone divorced remain single or return to their first marriage. One of those definitely wasn't going to be an option, and the other one didn't sound like a life I wanted to live forever.

I asked Billy and the elders of the church what they thought. They were full of grace, understanding, and wisdom about the situation. Life isn't perfect. It's messy. That old saying that cleanliness is next to godliness may be true, but I believe messiness is next to godliness, too. King David, the "man after God's own heart," was about as messy a man as ever lived. As close as he was to God, you would think that he wouldn't have been such a great sinner. You would logically think that a man who truly is close to God wouldn't be a murderer, liar, adulterer, polygamist, and warrior who killed many enemies. He shed so much blood that even God wouldn't let him build the temple in Israel. Yet, he is regarded as the greatest King to ever have lived. He is in the direct lineage of Jesus. I can't for the life of me understand how some church leaders today can draw such a hard line of morality in the sand and discount and disqualify those who stand on the wrong side of their line. David would not have made their cut. And David is just one example. There are many, many more.

This situation with Amanda was fairly messy. And it was what it was. But in that messiness, we both had peace and were excited to see what could come out of a relationship together. As my first winter in Minnesota came to a close, Amanda finished school and moved herself up to Dassel. She moved in with a sweet widow from our church, and we started dating. In a small town with very little to do, much of our dating was spent eating meals together. There really weren't many places to go, so we mostly just spent time across the dinner table from one another. It was across the table later that spring that we both acknowledged we wanted to marry each other, and two weeks later, we did just that. We had a small surprise wedding on June 13, 2010. We spent a total of two-hundred dollars on the entire wedding. That included rings. For Amanda's wedding ring, we found an antique spoon ring at an antique store that had a "D" inscribed on it. She later got the "D" from that ring tattooed on her wrist. I got a ring made of tungsten on Amazon. Amanda bought a simple white dress on sale at

Urban Outfitters. I wore khakis and a gray shirt. We wrote our own vows, too. I wrote mine in the form of a song:

"Sometimes I sit and wonder what you see in me
I'm a bit too old for you and a bit too heavy
But you look past my flaws and my insecurities
You bring out the best in me
I though I knew what love was so many years ago
But you, my dear, have shown me
There's so much that I don't know
I swear I won't forsake you, and faithful always be
You bring out the best in me
And all the years, I promise to bring out the best in you
Hold you close beside me through all that we'll go through
I'll build you up, not break you down, even if we disagree
You bring out the best in me
Our kids will never question whether daddy loves his wife
They'll see my love grow more for you
Each day throughout our lives
And when my last day comes, everybody will agree
That you brought out the best in me
And all the years, I promise to bring out the best in you
Hold you close to me darling, through all that we'll go through
I'll build you up, not break you down, this is my guarantee
You bring out the best in me."

And after everything I had been through up to this day to move my life forward—my time at the ranch, the journey to the Badlands, and the move up north—a new season of my life was beginning: a fresh start, a chance to be a better man. I was so young yet had lived through so much.

At only twenty-seven, I had been through a divorce. I had been through a foreclosure (related to the divorce). I had been through financial ruin. I had sold off nearly all that I had acquired as an adult at this point. I had moved so many times. I had lost my career, questioned my calling, and felt like I had no purpose. I moved to Colorado when I was twenty-five. I had spent my twenty-sixth year getting healthy, and during that year, I had moved up north. Now here I was turning twenty-seven, and I was so ready for what was next. Healthy. Whole. All that was lost, restored. And not only restored, but restored tenfold, hundred-fold, really.

They say divorce is like a death. It is. That relationship had become sick because I had been terminal for most of my life until that past year. I had never dealt with the trauma of my childhood. Some people say they carried scars, but I wasn't scarred from all we went through growing up. I wasn't scarred from my parents' divorce or my distant father. I wasn't scarred from living in twenty-two homes. I wasn't scarred from my mom's remarriage to a drug user or all of the stress and poverty we went through as kids. No scars on me. Scars would imply I had healed at some point and only had memories and stories. The reality is, until everything fell apart, I had no reason to heal. My cuts weren't even on the skin. They were deep inside of me, rooted into my very DNA. They had mutated me from who I was created to be to a terminal young adult who was emotionally and spiritually always on life support.

Life support is an interesting concept. You are literally being kept alive by something other than your own body. When I was eighteen, my actual body had been on life support. I had graduated high school in June while living in Germany. I had planned to go to an American college in Germany with a friend, but the time to go came and I ended up staying home. I honestly don't remember how the situation ended up that way, but it did. Good thing, too. In September, a month after I would have moved, I went to bed with a headache that I couldn't shake for days. And on the night of September 18, 2001, I had a brain aneurism. I had gone to bed, and my mother heard commotion in my bedroom soon after. She entered the room, and I was having a grand mal seizure. She yelled for my younger brother, who was fourteen at the time, and he came running into the room. The seizure started subsiding, and my eyes rolled back. He would literally slap me across the face, and I would come back and seize more.

It was exactly one week after 9/11, and our military base was completely locked down. It took forty-five minutes for a German ambulance to arrive at our house on the base. For forty-five minutes, I seized, and every time my eyes rolled back and I attempted to leave this world, my brother slapped me back into life. It was one of his proudest moments as a teenager, to slap his older brother over and over again.

I, of course, have only heard this story. I have no memory of this. What I remember was going to bed. I then remember opening my eyes and seeing a very tall ceiling with florescent lights. I remember feeling my body and being naked and in a robe. I looked to my left, and I saw one of our Army chaplains, Chaplain Arauco, who saw me look at him. He came running over to me. I tried to move but realized my body was hooked up to many machines. They had believed me to be in a coma, and they had machines on me to keep my brain stable. The odd thing though was that it was around three in the morning when I opened my eyes. I only had the seizure six hours ago. And at this point, there was no explanation as to what had happened.

The next day, and for the next month, I had every test the hospital could perform. I saw so many doctors, half surprised I had survived and the other half trying to find out exactly how I survived. They had concluded I had had a brain aneurism and that I must have had it my entire life sitting dormant, like a bomb. There was no reason for it bursting, it was just it's time. But I had survived it. And I had survived it with no permanent damage or side effects. There was one thing that was now attributed to the aneurism that had always been a mystery before. I do not have vision in my right eye. I have light, but not vision. It's hard to explain because I do see some things from my right eye, but it's not what I see in my left eye. It's as if I'm looking through a veiled kaleidoscope. The doctors believed that my eye misdeveloped in the womb and attributed it's misdevelopment to the aneurism that must have formed when I was in the womb as well. At least, this was their theory. And there I was, living a month of my eighteenth year in a clinic in Germany, being tested and observed. When I left the clinic near the end of October, I was given a clean bill of health. I had survived. And I had survived with nothing negative that was going to alter my life.

I had survived it all: my childhood, my divorce, all of the loss, and everything else I had walked through. I had been in a process of healing since the ranch, but what I thought was my heart healing was really the shedding of a dead shell. And I finally stepped out. I did so on my twenty-seventh birthday, the day before I married Amanda. I chose that day because I needed a defining moment to remember. I think we all need those defining moments, where we can see like a marker where we've been and remember where we've come from. I was in Iceland earlier this year, and Amanda and I kept seeing these rock piles randomly in the middle of nowhere spaced out along the roads and the open fields we passed. There are no trees in Iceland, so we could see these vertical pillars of rocks stacked repeating over and over as they shrank into the horizon. When we realized what they were, we were fascinated. These stone cairns were hundreds of years old and served as markers to tell the early explorers of Iceland where they had come from should they get lost in the snow and ice that far north on the globe.

I, too, had raised my own stone cairn in the north.

YELLOWSTONE

Time goes by so fast. This is a universal truth. You blink your eyes and a year goes by. Even today I have really great friends all over the country who I rarely speak with anymore. It's nothing personal; we're just all so busy. When we finally do connect, we're both always shocked that it's been so many months since we last spoke. I feel like the older I've gotten, the quicker time has accelerated. Amanda and I have been married ten years now, but it seemed like our small wedding was yesterday. I have the same feeling about Minnesota. We moved out of Dassel many years ago, but if I pulled into that little town today and pulled into the driveway of the house we lived in, I could easily walk back into our living room like we were only gone for the weekend. In many ways, our time in Minnesota was some of our best days. It was just the two of us back then, on our own schedule and pursuing our passions together.

Both Amanda and I are adventurers. We love to travel and explore new places and see new sights. Though we had gotten married in June, we planned our honeymoon in August. It wasn't your typical honeymoon that couples are expected to take the day after their wedding. We just planned a road trip. We also invited my brother Daniel and his fiancé Rachel to join us. The plan was Yellowstone. Daniel and Rachel would fly up to Minneapolis from Virginia Beach, and we'd spend a few days at our home in Dassel. Then, we'd load the car and head west. Once my mom got word of our trip, she decided that she and my youngest brother Joshua would come as well. Joshua was in high school, and the two of them would drive up from Colorado Springs and meet us there. So we were going to be six people in Yellowstone together for our honeymoon.

Yellowstone from our driveway was about a seventeen-hour drive. We were going to make the drive in two days. Once there, we'd stay for four days and then spend two days driving home. One of my favorite things to do is to plan trips. If a career as a travel agent was still viable, I would be so successful and fulfilled. Planning a trip involves a lot of research. You've got to determine the roads and route you're going to drive and figure out your stops along the way. There's a great website that's been around since the early days of the Internet called "Roadside America." It's a massive database of all the strange and insignificant things to see all over the country. Once I was driving across Nebraska with a friend and found a monument not too far from the interstate where two brothers, age fifteen and twelve, were pinned together by an arrow from a Sioux Indian attack in 1864. They actually survived the attack and were unpinned by a doctor. Both lived well beyond being pinned together, one dying middle aged and one becoming an old man. We stood at the stone monument in a cornfield. You will only find this kind of thing on Roadside America.

I tried to find anything of interest that I could for us to stop and see on the way to Yellowstone. The planned route would take us across the farmlands of Minnesota and hit I-90 where Iowa, Minnesota, and South Dakota all border one another. Then we'd drive across South Dakota and into Wyoming. Once we'd cross Wyoming, we'd hit Yellowstone. I was familiar with South Dakota, at least the west side. And I was familiar with Wyoming, at least the southern and eastern portions of the state. It was a very straight drive, and I-90 would take us the majority of the way. We loaded up the car with everything we needed to camp and hike Yellowstone and got going early in the morning.

Our first stop of the day would be the Corn Palace in Mitchell, South Dakota, recommended highly by Roadside America. We pulled off the interstate and into Mitchell, which was a very small town to boast such an odd attraction. Every year, the local corn harvest is artistically laid out into a design that covers the outside of a community center. The inside is just like any other civic center or gymnasium you'd find anywhere. But the outside is a shrine to America's greatest agricultural accomplishment, giving this basic brick building the honorable title of Corn Palace. I honestly expected more, which was becoming a theme of mine. Unrealistic expectations were a go-to distortion.

We are all a product of our environments. Our fears, insecurities, and even our worldview didn't manufacture themselves. They were created within us from all of the emotional, mental, or physical assaults we've survived. These things shape our personality. They shape how we process things that happen to us or around us in our life. We are taught to irrationally think. David Burns, author of *The Feeling Good Handbook*, lays out the ten cognitive distortions we all are prone to do:

- There's **mental filtering**, where you tend to filter things out of your conscious awareness.
- There's **jumping to conclusions**, where you tend to make irrational assumptions about people and circumstances.

- There's **personalization**, where you constantly take the blame for absolutely everything that goes wrong with our life.
- There's **all-or-nothing thinking**, where you only see the extremes of the situation.
- There's **overgeneralization**, where you conclude that one thing that happened to you once will occur over and over again.
- There's **disqualifying the positive**, where you transform neutral or even positive experiences into negative ones.
- There's **magnification and minimization**, where you look at your errors, fears, or imperfections and exaggerate or minimize their importance.
- There's **emotional reasoning**, where you take your emotions as evidence for the truth.
- There's **"should" statements**, where you try to motivate yourself by saying, "I should do this."
- There's **labeling and mislabeling**, where you have a tendency to create a completely negative self-image based on your errors.

We all do some or all of those things, and we must learn to identify them and call them out the moment they start happening. Grounding ourselves in truth is the only way to really live free. I've have spent almost my entire adult life fighting many of these distortions. One of the sharpest distortions in my quiver is jumping to conclusions. This is true of the way I predict the outcomes of situations and true of what I visualize things to be. My expectations are so easily distorted. Once I've imagined something in my head, it's hard to square up to the reality that may be vastly different. Places are like this for me. With my love for planning trips, I visualize every moment. I can see the places I'm going to visit and imagine their surroundings. It's almost like creating a fictional world. It's the shadow world, not in a sense that it's a dark world, but it's a 2D projection, not a 3D reality. Our own memories even exist in this world. There are actual studies and scientific evidences that prove that most of our memories have been fantasized and no longer represent reality in all of the details. They're in the shadow world. That certainly makes writing stories from memory difficult, as the stories become more philosophical and less factual.

The shadow world makes you feel like things are reality when in fact they're not. This is one of the many dangers of pornography. It's in 2D, which isn't real and cannot be touched or experienced. It's a shadow of something real, which is true intimacy. But true intimacy can only exist in reality. It has to be touched and experienced with all of our senses. Yet so many people are so easily trapped in the 2D, and it ruins their life. The biggest danger of the shadow world is that it's hard to unsee. The first time I saw a pornographic image at my youth group has forever been burned into my brain. I can't unsee it. I don't want to remember it, but I do. The same can be true of our fantasies about places or people before we get to know them. It all exists in the shadow world.

In the shadow world, I had made Rapid City a home it actually wasn't. I had made Dassel into a bigger city. I had made the Corn Palace much more grand, a kingdom in the prairies. But it's just a multipurpose arena in a little town in the middle of nowhere. We stayed in Mitchell long enough to take a picture in front of the palace, and then we were back on the road.

By the late afternoon, we had made it to the Badlands. It had been over a year since my inaugural trip to this place. My experience had been so powerful and moving here that I wanted to revisit and recreate the feelings of freedom I had found in the year prior. I actually would come to the Badlands again a few years later with Amanda and her brother, Danny. Each time I've been to the Badlands, I've always been moved by its beauty. It's always fun to watch other people love something you love as well. Seeing my family take in the beauty and sights of this special place was like reliving it again for the first time. We stopped along the same places I had been, walked the same trails I had walked, and saw the same canyons I had seen. Only this time, I was in a much different place. My life had been given a restart, and with that newness, I took in the Badlands with new eyes and enjoyed the wonders of its colors and canyons as if they were my first time.

We left the Badlands, did the honorary stop at Wall Drug, and eventually made it to a campsite in the Black Hills before sunset. We got our tents set up, got a fire going, and cooked dinner. My brother and I spent that evening sitting under the stars, catching up, and telling stories of our childhood. Many of our stories aren't fun or funny, but we make them that way or talk in disbelief about them. By now they've become legends to us, and honestly, who knows if they're even factual anymore. They're likely part of the shadow world of our memories.

The next morning, we got up with the sun and packed everything up into the car. We set out for a quick stop at Mount Rushmore and Devil's Tower and made our way out of the Black Hills. We stopped for lunch in Gillette, Wyoming, which at this point felt like New York City, despite having only twenty-thousand residents. After lunch, we continued toward Cody, where we would meet up with my mom and youngest brother for the night. As we crossed into western Wyoming, we entered the Bighorn National Forest. This was an absolutely beautiful drive through valleys, mountains, and canyons in the open wilderness. This area is full of switchbacks as you make your way across Bighorn.

As we were descending down into a valley, the steering wheel of the PT Loser became really stiff. We had to slow down significantly just to be able to turn the car around the switchbacks without going off the edge of the road and, ultimately, the edge of the cliff. I thought maybe it was just me; after all I had been driving for two days. I pulled the car over, and Daniel took the wheel as we continued driving. When the next switchback came, he had the same experience. The power steering was definitely out. We were able to make our way through Bighorn and onto Cody just in time to set up camp. Power steering isn't exactly mission-critical to driving a car, but you'd better have some strength and determination to drive the mountains without it. The PT Cruiser wasn't going to leave us on the side of the road on this trip, but it was going to make driving a little more difficult. We didn't have time to stop for hours or days to get this thing fixed, and we figured the worst of the drive was over since we made it through Bighorn. The drive back would be a different route and a lot flatter. We'd go home through eastern Montana and North Dakota, which is about as flat and straight a drive you could ask for. We could do this.

We met up with my mom and Joshua, and all caught up. It had been several months since we had all been in the same place at once, as we were living in three different parts of the country. Daniel was on the east coast in Virginia, I was in Minnesota, and mom and Joshua were in Colorado. We enjoyed each other's company that evening and finalized our plan to head into Yellowstone in the morning.

As someone who takes the time to research and plan a trip, I had a pretty awesome agenda laid out for us in Yellowstone. In our brief time there, we were going to be able to see every major site, do some beautiful hikes, camp at the best campgrounds, and really explore one of America's most iconic National Parks. I had bought a book that diagramed, explained, and rated every trail in Yellowstone, and there are many trails. I had gone through this book and read the descriptions, studied the maps, and planned out hikes on the trails that I was most excited to see. As we entered Yellowstone from the east entrance, we only had a short drive to one of the first hikes I had planned for us. This particular hike was through a vast prairie field, into the forest, and onto an open area with a secluded stream and grand mountains on the horizon. There were likely going to be herds of bison grazing in the fields by the stream. We were going to see this land as it once was— no evidences of man. This is what the National Parks are all about, preserving a way of life before we interrupted it. We parked our cars and set out for the hike. This was going to be the entire first half of the day, nearly four hours. We should make it out in time to grab lunch at one of the many visitor center restaurants in the park and continue on our way.

First we crossed the field. During the entire hike across the field, my mom kept talking about grizzly bears and how prevalent they are in Yellowstone. This was a true statement, but I had taken the precautionary measures to keep us as safe as possible. In my bag I had packed a tambourine, and with every step, there was a jingle. This was one of the ways you could discourage wildlife from coming near you, as most of the wildlife (including bears) aren't interested in interacting with humans. In the event that things went south, I had a can of bear spray. And worst-case scenario, we'd just run and the slowest of us would take one for the team. Amanda had been a cross-country runner, and I was pretty quick, so I knew at least the two of us would make it.

Once we entered the woods, my mom and my brothers were all hyped up about grizzly bears. Every broken stick on the trail was because a bear had stepped on it. They were hearing bears move around the woods as if we were now in a horror movie about a sleuth of bears who conspired together to kill humans in the forest. My family made it seem like the scene toward the end of *Jurassic Park: The Lost World* where they're all running from the dinosaurs and the one guy is shouting "Don't go into the tall grass!" In the movie, a pack of raptors attacked and nearly killed them all. I basically had my mom yelling "Don't go into the woods!" So rather than hike this trail I had so meticulously selected and planned for, my mom and my brothers, terrified of encountering a bear, opted to turn around and head back to the car. Amanda and I had no choice but to keep the peace and return with them.

My plans were unraveling quickly. Since we didn't complete the hike, we were several hours ahead of schedule. This meant we weren't having lunch where I had planned, as we'd be past the restaurant. It meant that we wouldn't get to Old Faithful near-eruption and we'd be spending time waiting around, which isn't efficient when you're trying to cover a massive park in only a few days. The plans fell apart play by play. What was once my precisely planned journey through Yellowstone had become my mom's "just wing it" vacation. A family cannot have two alphas, and she quickly asserted her dominance the moment we entered the park. The rest of Yellowstone was basically her setting the agenda. Yes, we saw most of what I had planned for us to see, but it wasn't my trip. It wasn't what I had spent months planning.

You know that old saying, "If you want to make God laugh, tell Him about your plans?" This phrase was coined by the great theologian Woody Allen. Of course Woody Allen isn't known for theology, and this phrase makes God seem like a vindictive prankster who takes joy in disrupting your vision and preparation for things. I don't think this is how God operates. But there is a truth that things don't always go according to our plans. In a moment, all we worked and planned for can fall apart. It did in Yellowstone, and while it was a fairly trivial plan to fall apart, the principle is the same for any plans no matter how important or insignificant. Murphy's law says that "anything that can go wrong will go wrong." This is just as true of plans.

Amanda and I had a major plan that went wrong during our first year of marriage. When we got married, I was twenty-seven years old, and she was twenty-one. We both wanted children, and I wanted that to happen sooner than later. I didn't want to be an old dad. While my parents had absolutely no idea what they were doing when they had me at twenty-two and twenty-one, today I can appreciate their youthfulness. A lot of couples get married, have several years alone together, and then start trying for children. If I waited several years, I'd be in my thirties before having kids, and that meant I'd be in my fifties when they became adults, and I want to spend as much time as possible with my children as babies, kids, and adults. Amanda wanted to be a mom just as much as I wanted to be a dad, and we began trying for children soon after we were married. We thought we'd be pregnant by Christmas and parents by the next summer or so.

But Christmas came and went. No pregnancy after several months. Then summer came. No pregnancy after a year. We weren't sure what was going on, and Internet searches only gave me anxiety. Was it me? Was it her? Was it able to be fixed? What if we can't have children? Then the distortions began.

"Of course this is happening to me." Overgeneralization.

"This is my fault, because I failed at my first marriage. I'm cursed." Personalization. Labeling.

And those distortions can really mess you up because if you tell yourself something enough, you start to believe it. You can be as healthy of a person imaginable, but if you let distortions like this into your life and do not have a corrective voice to check them, you'll quickly descend into a valley of irrational thoughts, and in that valley you won't be able to clearly see reality. You'll get tunnel vision. And as the walls close in and that valley narrows, you'll feel as anxious as ever.

The best way to check a distortion is with truth. The quickest way to truth in our situation was to go see a doctor, so that's what we did.

After some testing, we found out that Amanda had polycystic ovary syndrome, or PCOS for short. The good news is that this isn't terribly uncommon, and many women with PCOS have biological children. There were fertility medicines that helped women with PCOS get pregnant, and our doctor was fairly optimistic that given our age, we'd be having a baby within the next year. PCOS is when your ovaries are covered in small cysts, and therefore your ovaries don't release eggs every month in a normal cycle. The eggs are essentially choked out. This explained why Amanda had never had normal periods and sometimes missed a period, giving us false hope that she was pregnant over and over during that past year.

The doctor gave Amanda a prescription for Clomid, which helps with ovulation. The idea was that Clomid would help release the eggs and thus increase our chances of having a baby. After that first year of nothing happening, we were feeling good and optimistic with the hope that we'd be having a baby with the help of Clomid. The first month was unsuccessful. The second month was the same, as was the third and onto the sixth. And exactly one year later, we were sitting across from our doctor in Minneapolis. She told us at this point, she did not believe we would have biological children unless we wanted to try in vitro fertilization. As we saw the costs associated with IVF, we knew it was something we wouldn't be able to do. Also, it wasn't a guaranteed success, and while many people have had success with IVF, there are also many who spent a lot of money and never had a successful pregnancy. It was just too much risk for us in that moment. And while we were making it financially, I worked for a small church in a small town, and Amanda worked for a small salon in the small town next door. We didn't have the income to really make IVF an option.

Our family plans were changing. Just like the disrupted plans in Yellowstone, change is so frustrating and disappointing. I never got to see that stream. And now it's looking like we're never going to have our own children. There is a type of heartbreak and pain that only comes from infertility that I'm not sure anyone who hasn't been there before can empathize with and appreciate. Today, when I meet people who have had similar journeys, I understand that pain they describe because I've felt it. We watched friends get pregnant and have kids while we were trying, month after month. We even saw people get married, get pregnant, and have kids while we were still trying. It's a pain that comes back around every month, too. For two years, we had a reminder every month that weren't going to be parents.

If you asked me if I was a dog or cat person, I would tell you that I am a big dog person. Not a big dog person, as in, I'm big on dogs. What I mean is, I like big dogs. To me, the best dogs are over sixty pounds. Amanda never had a dog growing up but had cats, and during the month-to-month crushing of infertility, she was desperate for something to love. Our friend Tommy had gone deer hunting as the weather was cooling off and Minnesota deer season had begun. Instead of returning home with a buck one morning, he came home with two kittens he had found at his deer stand. Tommy and his family had a special affection for animals and pets, and rather than let these two kittens find their way out in the woods, he brought them home to find them homes. One of those kittens ended up at our house, and he was so helpful in meeting our parenting need. We named him Crunchy. Amanda's cat growing up was named Chewy. Crunchy seemed like a fitting name. And I was resolute that if I was ever going to have a cat, it had to be an all-black cat since they at least look like panthers, which are definitely over sixty pounds. Crunchy, our all-black cat, joined our family in the midst of a very hard season for us and brought some healing into our house.

THE BARISTA

M innesota has been a fresh start. It was a new beginning. A resurrection and a rebirth. Before moving there, and even soon after being there, I would dream of the new community I would surround myself with: new friends to share new experiences with and new people to have accountability and chase my dreams with. But there was that distortion of "jumping to conclusions" again. I figured with the move up north and then with getting married, Amanda and I would have an awesome friend circle, the kind you see in the stock images of people hanging out at someone's house, or having a fourth of July party, or eating together at a restaurant. But this was in the shadow world, not my real world.

The community at Dassel just wasn't that group from the stock images. In fact, nearly everyone in our community was part of a larger and local family. Many of them had kids, and some of our closest friends in the area were nearly our parents' age. This was a double-edged sword because while we had access to incredible wisdom and maturity, we didn't have anyone living our lifestyle. We were the only childless couple under forty at our church, and our church was our primary source of community in our lives. And while the local large families were sure to include us as if we shared their Swedish and Norwegian last names, the truth is, we didn't. We were still outsiders. Community simply wasn't going as planned. It wasn't what I imagined it would be.

But we made it work as best we could. My primary community has always been around music and creatives, and I had created that. I had begun leading the music and worship for a regional women's conference called Best Life, and for that, I needed a band. My band was a perfect illustration of where our community was. I had grabbed the best musicians I could find who were like-minded and available. When you see a band, they generally look like they belong together. They have a commonality through their age, appearance, or vibe. Not my band. We looked like a foster family. There was me, who was in my late twenties. There was Amanda, who was in her mid-twenties. We had a similar vibe. But then there was Steve, a local Youth Pastor. He was in his forties and was from Iowa. Then there was Jim, who was also in his forties and was a local preacher, the kind who could bring down fire and brimstone. He was well over six-feet tall and looked like our security more than our keyboard player. There was Roberto, our shy and quiet Hispanic drummer. There was Jessie, who was in his late thirties and was a tired father of four. And last there was James, who was only a teenager but was the best guitarist in the area. Together we wrote songs, recorded music, and played many live events around the state, from Best Life Conferences to church events to the Sonshine Festival and even the Minnesota State Fair. And this was our community, no one where we were in life.

It's kind of hard to go through life without someone at least somewhat remotely close to where you are in life. Our time in Minnesota, though wonderful and foundational for us as a couple, was fairly lonely. It was just the two of us more often than not. I once heard Ian Morgan Cron speaking at a conference from Psalm 92 about how, when we plant ourselves in the right place, we will grow and flourish. It really stirred me to ask myself if I was planted in the right place. I think that's a question everyone needs to ask themselves, not just once but often. I ask myself that question at least once a year these days. I take inventory of my life and evaluate where things are against the vision I have for myself and my family. I personally want to make my time matter the most, and to do so I've got to be in a place both physically and mentally to make that happen. If where I am in any given moment isn't allowing me to produce the best results from and for my life, I'm open to change. I think we all should be. Change can be scary and intimidating, but it only seems that way because of our distortions. If you can actually and factually improve your life through making some changes, the only thing that prevents you from doing so are usually the distortions.

My father and stepmother had come to visit us in our last fall in Minnesota. Amanda and I had made it public earlier in the year that we were going to start planning to adopt, domestically. We had begun saving money, fundraising, and taking the necessarily classes and training to adopt. We were taking trips to Minneapolis, working with an adoption organization to get the process going as quick as we could afford. When my father came up, they gave us a sizable check toward our adoption. This was a pretty impactful moment, but what made a greater impact was something he said to me while visiting. My dad and I are good friends, but we've never really been close. I take his words as a source of wisdom or practicality. And something he said moved me, which was rare in our relationship. While during his last couple of days at our house, he said:

"You know, if you stayed here for the next twenty years, you'll probably be doing the same thing then that you are doing right now."

Those words really sank in. He was absolutely right. The lifestyle of this town was slow, and the work was fairly slow and easy as well. I had a great routine and had proven that I was a hard worker that didn't need micromanagement. Things were really routine and predictable in Dassel. They always had been, and they likely always will be. That's why people move to and live in small towns, with the slow, quiet, routine, and predictable lifestyles. I had spent four years in Minnesota caring for and leading that church. Billy had left after my first year. The next year I led the church solo. The third year, we hired a guy I met a few years before. I think I was more excited about having a young guy like myself to work with, but it wasn't working out. And before my fourth year anniversary, I had taken inventory and done my evaluation, and it was time for a change. New plans.

In the winter before we moved, I had been in contact with a church in the Phoenix area of Arizona. The church was significantly larger than the church I was at. I was at a church of around a hundred and twenty or so, and this church had been running around five thousand. It was also in a suburb of Phoenix called Surprise, which had exploded in growth in the decade before, and the entire city was basically new shopping, new restaurants, and new homes. It was sunny nearly every day of the year, and there was no snow. It was the literal opposite of the old and small town of Dassel I was living in. The job was in the church's music department, mainly leading their audio team. It wasn't a pastoral job like I had in Minnesota, as it was a much more technical job. After years of being involved in people's lives in a small town, I needed some respite from pastoral work. Also, I was beginning to get bookings for my own music much more often on the west coast. I had a growing network in Southern California, and Phoenix would make that part of the country incredibly accessible.

The church asked us to come visit for a weekend that winter. They even told us that if anything, they'd make sure we had a good trip and got to enjoy the break from winter. With several feet of snow on the ground and temperatures below freezing in Minnesota, that sounded like a really great proposition. They booked flights for Amanda and I, and we were ready to go visit Surprise.

But before we did, we had to have a conversation with the elders in Dassel. We had a meeting once a month where we had dinner and talked church business, and that was coming up quickly. Telling them I was interviewing somewhere else was a little risky because anytime you tell an employer that you're interviewing somewhere else, you're basically signing your letter of resignation. Even if things didn't work out in Surprise, there was likely no going back once I shared with them that I was exploring another opportunity. In the church world, since our jobs are so personally connected with the lives of those in the church, this topic can be even more sensitive. While I technically only reported to and worked for the elders of the church, in many ways all church employees work for the entire congregation. At least, oftentimes people in the congregation felt that way. And once you let them down, it's hard to go back.

But as hard as it was going to be to tell the elders that I was interviewing somewhere else, I knew it was the right thing to do. I could have easily just asked for the weekend off and told them Amanda and I were taking a personal trip. But if I took the job in Surprise, I didn't want them to feel deceived. I also wanted to give them a chance to process what me leaving would look like for the church. I carried much of the day-to-day operation and was heavily invested in the lives of many people who attended. The elders would need to walk people through us leaving, and that was going to be hard. When we gathered together for our dinner, I told them that in three weeks Amanda and I would be traveling to the Phoenix area and interviewing for a new position. They each reacted true to themselves. Dan was happy for me and affirmed my gifting. Galen was surprised, with a bit of disbelief on his face. He wished me luck and offered his support. Randy really didn't say anything, as he rarely did in awkward situations or potential transitions. I wasn't the first staff member to interview somewhere else and leave. And then there was Tom, who had some reservations within but supported me in the process. I could see he was thinking things but was not saying them at the moment. Tom asked if we could get lunch, and the following day, we went to a local pizza place. Lunch was normal, and we didn't once speak about Phoenix. As we were driving back to the church office, Tom finally said what had been on his mind.

"You know, Dave, you like to be in charge."

Truth. In the months before, the elders and I had taken a leadership retreat. While I worked for them and reported to them, for that weekend I had actually brought the agenda and led the discussion through the church's business. That was my weekend, and we got a lot done. It was really the first time I had taken charge. It was the first time I felt like I could take charge, like I had been trusted and given authority. Most of the time, we already have the things we need, like trust and authority, but we don't take it because of distortions, like emotional reasoning. I don't feel like I'm trusted, and therefore I'm not trusted. I don't feel like I can actually lead this, and therefore I cannot lead this. Our own limitations are in the shadow world. They're 2D projections, not 3D realities. Tom continued:

"People that like to be in charge have a hard time working for other people. It sounds like this job you're interviewing for is pretty far down in the organization, and I don't think you're going to be happy there."

Tom was right—it was several layers down from the decision-makers of the church, those who were in charge. There was the board, followed by the Lead Pastor. Reporting to him was the Worship Pastor, and reporting to the Worship Pastor would be me, part of the worship staff. What Tom saw as a problem, I honestly saw as a blessing. I was happy to be down in the organization, to not matter too much to the operation. I had been so critical for many years to the business of the church, and the idea of not being really important sounded great. I was tired of being "on." Everyday. "On."

I can't speak much to work outside of the church world, but I'll tell you something that is very true inside the church world. If you work for a church, there is no "off time." Of course there's "time off," but there is a difference between "time off" and "off time." Let me explain.

Time off is something universal that everyone who works receives. Let's say you work from eight to five every day, then realistically you're *off* from five until eight the following day. Granted, fewer and fewer people actually leave their work at work these days, but logically that is how it's supposed to work. You work eight hours a day, and you're off for sixteen hours. Also, you have weekends or days off. During these days, you get an extended break to rest and spend time doing the things you love. In the traditional sense, you get the weekend. All day Saturday and all day Sunday is your time off. And hopefully, you get even more extended time off for vacations or staycations, whatever you're feeling and into. During those times, you have a week or more off to rest, enjoy your family or your hobbies, and be recharged and refreshed to continue your work.

I've always gotten time off just like anyone else in the marketplace and economy. I have a work day, and then I go home. Same with my work week. As a church leader, I don't get traditional weekends, but

I've always had a couple of days off a week, equally with the rest of society. And I've always had vacation times and extended time off as I've scheduled, planned for, and needed. Nearly everyone who works in the economy in some way or another has some time off.

But off time isn't universal to the economy. Off time does not easily come to those who work jobs that have publicity. In the most obvious sense, politicians and celebrities don't get off time. A big reason I believe so many of them are caught up in scandals or drama is because they don't know how to carry themselves always being "on." This is also true of pastors and church workers and sadly why so many pastors get caught up in scandals themselves. There is a long list of men and women who have gotten in trouble doing things that I'm certain were motivated by their distortions, not their logical processing of things. I don't want to drop names, but just search for "pastor scandal," and you're going to find nearly as many horrible situations with pastors and church leaders as you'll find of politicians and celebrities.

Anyone who works in the public doesn't get "off time." We constantly have to manage ourselves. It's almost as if pastors and church workers need a full-time public relations staff member, like politicians and celebrities have. Instead, many of us have learned to be our own PR. And many of us suffer for it. Managing your image can rot you from the inside out, as you learn to have split personalities and how to manipulate people. No one sets out wanting to live this way. You just die a little day after day, year after year, until the person you are is not the person you wanted to be. And the worst part is that no one knows the real you because you've so tactfully controlled your public image for so many years.

It's tough never having off time. For instance, right now I'm sitting in a coffee shop very early in the morning working on this manuscript.

My go-to drink at this coffee shop is a medium Americano with four shots of espresso and light water. I like coffee to taste like coffee. I don't use sugar or cream, just black and strong. But imagine with me for a moment that my drink order was wrong. Let's say when I went back up to the counter, the barista was having a bad morning and rolled his eyes and gave me an attitude, like it was me that did something wrong. He then cues my drink up in the order to be remade, but let's say they're really busy and it's now number eleven in the line. I'm feeling frustrated. I'm feeling like as a consumer, I have paid for a little better experience than this.

So what should I do? Even if I wasn't a pastor or church worker, I honestly would probably not say or do anything. But the point I'm making is that I don't feel like I even *can* do anything. Follow me here. Let's say I ask him to see his manager. Anytime you ask someone in retail or services to see their manager, they know something is up and you're likely going to complain about something. This is why in reality I often ask to see a manager when service or experiences are exceptionally great, and I complement their workers. I love seeing the look on their faces because unfortunately compliments are rare in any industry.

But let's say I ask the barista to see his manager. There are three potential responses within the barista. First is apathy. He could truly not care. Second is anxiety. He could feel anxious about what I'm asking to see the manager for. He knows it's him. Maybe he knows that if he messes up one more time, he could lose his job. The third and final potential outcome is pushback, and he gets confrontational with me. I'll acknowledge that this is the most unlikely outcome, but it's still on the list because it happens. So right here, we've created a scenario where all of the potential outcomes are not going to be positive interactions with me:

- If he's apathetic, he could see me as annoying or frustrating.
- If he's anxious, he could have fear because of me.
- If he gets confrontational, he could become assaultive toward me in speech or worse.

I am a public figure in my community. Whether he knows me or not, every single person in my community is a potential client. Any church I would ever work for must be a nondiscriminatory house for all people, so anyone I meet in my community is someone I could invite. It's not even just the individual, but their entire network of family and friends are my potential clients too. My goal isn't just to get someone through our doors, but I want them to be so in love with their experience and the organization that they go out and bring others into it as well. This is the beginning of how we share the Gospel. We have to get people into the room first.

And I'm on the platform every week; they are going to see me, even if I do not see them. This is true whether you're at a church of fifteen or fifteen thousand. If you work at a church, you're a public figure. So as a public figure, what are my options with the barista? If he's a potential client, and his network is full of potential clients, what should I do with my frustrations at my less-than-stellar experience in the coffee shop? I don't want him feeling annoyed, anxious, or confrontational. I don't want that for anyone. And I especially don't want that for someone that is potentially going to be looking toward me for any spiritual guidance. Maybe he attends my church, and I've just never seen him. Maybe his family attends. Maybe in six years, he's going to walk through the doors for the first time in a life crisis, see me, and remember that experience in the coffee shop. And he'll turn around and walk away.

So I can't say anything, even if I wanted to, because I am "on" as a church leader. And while this story is so small and kind of stupid, it's the kind of thing that I have to think about every day. I have to think about how I appear in public. I have to think about how I drive around in the city. I have to think about the beverages in my shopping cart or what I might order in a restaurant. I have to think about the way I joke around, the way I use sarcasm, and the way I carry myself even when I'm just goofing off with friends. I have to do this with my closest friends who attend my church, as well as the strangers who I may never meet. I never have off time in my day-to-day life. I am always on.

The church in Arizona was so large, and my role so small that I could disappear. And that sounded wonderful. That's because when you think of ministry as a job like any other job, you think about on and off times. But ministry isn't a job. It's freedom from having to get a job. I used to believe that like any other job in the economy, my paycheck as a pastor was a result of my work, meaning that if I worked hard and produced results, I'd have job security. All jobs are created out of revenue generated, after all. So by working hard and doing a good job, revenue for the church will increase (or at least maintain), and I'd be compensated for my work. And while it's true that even church work is paid out from revenue generated, the compensation comes with a completely different message.

In ministry, you aren't solely paid for a job well done. You're paid to have your needs met, so you can give your time to the work of the church rather than having to have job in the economy. Collectively, the people of the church are giving toward your livelihood, normally through a board of overseers, elders, or whatever a local church government looks like. They are saying with the dollars they give that they believe in you, and they think your time is better spent on behalf of the church rather than having to work in the economy. They voted for you every week by faithfully taking care of the church, returning the tithe of ten percent to the Lord, and giving their offerings. It was a weekly vote of confidence. It was a weekly ask that I would always be "on" and available. As far as I can tell from the Bible, the only times Jesus had off was when he withdrew into a place of solitude to pray or rest. Yet even then, in times when he probably needed to be off the most, he was still on.

In Matthew 14, Jesus, upon hearing of the execution of his cousin John, went out of a boat to cross the Sea of Galilee and be alone. It says he we went "privately to a solitary place." He went to have some off time. In the next sentence, it says "but the crowds had heard." The word "but" means that Jesus was about to be interrupted. The crowds then "followed him on foot from the towns." Jesus wasn't going to have that off time after all. And I love what it says next—that Jesus saw the crowds: "he had compassion on them, and healed their sick." What happened next is the famous story of Jesus feeding the five thousand miraculously with only fives loaves of bread and two fish, all from interrupted off time.

When Paul says in his first letter to the Corinthians in Greece that he "died daily," I wonder what he meant. As a first-generation pastor in the church, I'm sure he was experiencing the weight and demand people place on their spiritual leaders. Maybe some or all of this weight is self-inflicted, but it's still there nonetheless. And everyday all church leaders must die to themselves, and their wills, and their desires, for the sake of Jesus. When I'm wronged by the barista, or anyone else as a consumer, I die daily. When someone is upset with me, even if irrationally, I say I'm sorry and I restore my relationship with them because I die daily. I wish I had understood this principle earlier in my life and ministry because it could have prevented a lot of heartaches and headaches over the years.

The Whiteout

We stepped onto our plane in Minneapolis when it was four degrees outside. We stopped off the plane in Phoenix at seventy-four degrees. It was gray and overcast in Minneapolis. It was completely sunny in Phoenix. Rather than icicles hanging down from our roof, palm trees were reaching up to the sky. And the church seemed just as great as the weather. It was huge. It was well-paying. It offered me some freedom and flexibility. And to make matters even better, Arizona had some adoption assistance programs that Minnesota didn't have. Through an organization in Minneapolis, we were saving toward a goal of twenty thousand dollars for adoption in Minnesota. In Arizona, it seemed like we would need around half of that to adopt a baby. All of this made for a very promising situation, and we decided that we would take the job and move our life to the Valley of the Sun.

Telling the elders at the church in Dassel was hard, but they knew it was coming at this point. When I shared with them that I was interviewing somewhere else, they knew at that point I would likely be leaving. I worked with both churches to make the transition happen in a single month. We would wrap up business and prepare the church in Dassel as best we could and then make the move to Phoenix. We began our goodbye tour, visiting families as we could over the next month to sit with them and share the journey our life was on. We received support from nearly everyone. It was a great experience: to be affirmed, loved, and believed in.

Near the close of winter on a freezing Saturday, we loaded up the moving truck and our car. I was going to drive the moving truck, and Amanda was going to drive our car with Crunchy. My mother flew up to help us pack and make the drive with us, sharing the driving responsibilities of the car with Amanda. Between the two of them, one could keep Crunchy in their lap and the other could drive. The next day on Sunday morning, the church did something really special for us. Tom spoke about our time there and what we meant to them. Then the entire church surrounded us, making a circle around us, and prayed over us and our future. It was emotional. These people meant so much to us. And although we were outsiders to this community, we had found a place among them over our four years there. Our time there was only temporary. But most things are. Temporary doesn't mean unimportant or unimpactful. Dassel, the people, the elders, and the church had such a great impact on me.

Seventeen hundred miles. That's how far it was from Dassel to Surprise. They weren't easy miles, either. It was an incredibly difficult drive. It was winter, and we drove across a lot of snowy states: Minnesota to Nebraska and then toward Colorado. As we made it toward the end of Nebraska, we found a place along the interstate and called it a night. There was a sign hanging over the entrance to the gas station next door that said "You Are Nowhere." I believed it. When we got up the next morning, we started out for Colorado. It had been a long time since I was last here. As we drove into Denver, I would only be an hour or so from the ranch, but personally, I couldn't be further from the man I was when I climbed Red Nose those many years before. And my life today looked so different than it did back then.

The plan was solid. Since we had such a long drive and we were going to need to stop for breaks anyway, I had strategically planned some places to stop. We'd cross the Rockies, get into Utah, and then take 191 south, stopping at Arches National Park and the city of Moab. I had wanted to see the desert landscapes of Utah for so long. The fact that our route was going to pass right through these places felt like destiny. God's favor. We were going to be moving into our rental house in Arizona in a couple of days, and I had planned our drive to get us to the house right on time to unload the truck before I'd start orientation the following day. It was a three-day drive. On day one, we'd drive to the end of Nebraska. On day two, we'd arrive at Arches in the afternoon and stay in Moab. On day three, we'd arrive in Phoenix by sundown. And on day four, I'd have my first day for orientation.

Day one went as planned. Then day two started. We got into the Rockies on I-70, and I was really enjoying the drive. Even from the interstate, the mountains are beautiful. Gray mountains were covered in snow, and the landscape monochromatic as if I was watching a classic black-and-white movie through my windshield. As we approached Silverthorne, we entered a long tunnel through a large mountain. When we entered the tunnel, the sky was blue and the air was clear. The roads were smooth and well maintained, something I had grown familiar with living in Minnesota. I'm from the southeast, where an inch of snow shuts down schools for a week and people literally die in car accidents. Yet in Minnesota, or Colorado, and all of the other snowy states, they know what they're doing with roads, so I had no fears driving same as I would in the middle of summer through the Rockies.

Near the end of the tunnel, the daylight was nearly blinding. It was like staring wide-eyed into a flashlight in a dark room. Squinting, I slowed the truck down a little as brake lights began to illumine the walls of the tunnel, the red lights glowing on the dark interior rock walls as if a concert was about to begin. Surely, a show had begun. Mother Nature was putting on a tremendous show in the form of a blizzard just on the other side of the tunnel. With no warning, we emerged from the tunnel into a snowstorm. Whiteout. The road disappeared underneath our tires. Hazard lights were blinking, and their faint pulsing was all anyone could see of each other's vehicles. No one could pull over or stop because no one could see the road. To make matters worse, we were descending the mountain, and gravity was accelerating our vehicles along with the ice and snow. Since we didn't know what to expect with mobile phone service, we had picked up some walkie-talkies that allowed us to communicate between the two cars. I was wearing mine on the seatbelt across my chest, and I grabbed it and asked Amanda and my mom if they were ok. I had lost sight of them in the whiteout. They radioed back and said they were fine, just trying to stay safe. So was I.

At the bottom of the mountain, traffic on I-70 came to a stop. Some people consider traffic stopped when things just slow down. This was a total and complete stop. No one was moving or going anywhere. I assumed there was an accident or something, or maybe the road had become impassable with the blizzard. After nearly an hour of sitting in the snow, our cars nearly becoming buried under ice, we finally started moving. Only we were not moving toward Utah. They were diverting us off the interstate into Silverthorne. As we approached the exit, we saw that several tractor trailers had collided and covered the interstate with wreckage. No one was going any further. As the cars and trucks came off the interstate, hotel parking lots began to fill up. We pulled into a hotel, went inside, and quickly got a room. By the evening when

I came down to the hotel lobby, I saw people setting up for the night on the lobby floors, with the hotel staff bringing cots, blankets, and pillows as they had them to accommodate people for the night. I was so grateful we came in when we did, and that we would at least have a bed and a bathroom for the night.

Due to the whiteout, we didn't have time the following day to stop at Arches. In fact, we had to drive straight to Phoenix, only stopping for bathroom breaks and quick meals. We made it into Arizona and drove across the Navajo Nation, one of the saddest places I had seen in the United States. Out in the red desert in Arizona is poverty that you wouldn't recognize in our country. And along the highway, glass shines like glitter from broken bottles. It broke my heart seeing this. It reminded me of how good my life actually was. We pulled into Surprise late that evening, exhausted from the long drive that day. Nearly eight-hundred miles straight. That night we unloaded what we needed from the truck. The following morning, we unloaded the rest and did our best to quickly settle into the new house.

Change. That was our theme. Like Yellowstone, my plans for this trip had changed. Our plans to be parents of our own children had changed. Our future for my career had changed. All things in life are subject to disruption. We've got to become comfortable with change. This is especially true of my generation and upcoming future generations. While my grandfather lived in the same town of Warsaw and went to the same church on the same street he grew up with his entire life, I have never known nor will I ever know that kind of consistency. You likely never will either. Change has to be welcomed and embraced without the distortions. Life has to be seen and considered not in the 2D shadow world, but in the 3D real world—the world you can touch, taste, and experience. And change is part of the real world. In my prior life in Charlotte with my ex, I had written a song about my relationship with change. I was processing the changes I knew were coming but hadn't arrived yet:

"Two thing that are for sure in life
That you will die and you will live through change
And nothing is promised but these
No, nothing is sacred, not even your name
For your name can change with just a paper
And you life can change with just a word
And your heart can change because of sadness
And your mind change because of things you have heard
Nothing is how it used to be, they say
I'm told that things will not remain
There are cries from the hearts that are broken
There are cries from the poor and the pained
There are cries from the child left unspoken
Crying out his fathers name
In the land of change
And you and me we're gonna be different
We're different because of who we are
Even more than this we have lived differently
We carry different battles and scars
And we are not who we used to be, they say
We've changed for better, for worse
Every heart in every man longs to know and understand
Why the man can't comprehend
the things that make peace in this land
Every cell and DNA, that makes us fit to fight to stay
Is longing for consistency, but consistency's a dream."

Arizona

O ut of the freezer, into the frying pan. That's what it's like moving from the coldest state in the continental US to the hottest. We had arrived in Surprise, Arizona, right at the beginning of spring, and it was already the equivalent of the summers in Minnesota. We traded our winter coats for shorts and t-shirts, our snow boots for sandals. We traded a yard with green grass and a high-yielding vegetable garden for rocks. Literally, rocks. The house we were renting had rocks instead of any grass or plants. In fact, I once got fined by the local homeowners association because some weeds had come up through the rocks and I hadn't killed them fast enough. This place did not want anything to grow.

New job, new routines. In Dassel, I didn't clock my hours or keep records of my coming and going. I had proven that I worked hard and produced results, and I was trusted with my time. At my new job in Surprise, my time was tracked by my key fob into the building. They knew when I came and when I went. Keeping hours was never a problem for me, but coming from an atmosphere of total freedom and flexibility to this new place where my daily activity was tracked took a little getting use to. It was a fair trade, though. Here in Surprise I worked for a large church that had a beautiful campus in a sunny and modern city. And I had some anonymity. In Dassel, I once had someone bang on my door at seven in the morning asking me for a few hundred dollars to help with rent. I lived in a parsonage, which is a house owned by the church and usually next door to the building, and everyone in the town knew where I lived. It never failed. Every week someone stopped by, most of them not even from our church, looking for financial help and handouts. I had to explain so many times that I didn't have cash on hand to give them from the church and that we had a process for assistance that they would need to follow. I love people, and I love helping people. But these kinds of situations where random people would literally knock on my door at their own leisure had really worn me thin.

But not in Surprise. No one from this church or this community would know where I lived. I had rented a house in a huge neighborhood with thousands of homes. I wouldn't have to worry about anyone just showing up. One of my biggest fears in Minnesota had always been someone showing up when I wasn't home and getting violent with Amanda. When I was in college, I heard of a pastor in North Carolina whose wife was murdered at their home by someone showing up, demanding money from the church, and then taking his family hostage. This story horrified and terrified me. It also broke my heart because unfortunately it wasn't a cautionary tale but a true story. It gave me so much anxiety when we lived in the parsonage beside the church in Minnesota.

On one Sunday afternoon in Dassel, we had friends over after church, grilling lunch on the back porch. I saw a car pull into the church parking lot and up to the building and watched two young men get out of the car. They could see me on the back porch, and I could see them, plain as day. I watched one bust in the church's back door and run inside. I didn't realize what was going on right away, but I kept watching, with the one who stayed beside the car watching me. The other guy came running out with my guitar, which he had grabbed from the stage, threw it in their back seat, and together they quickly pulled out of the parking lot. They had just broken into the church and stolen my guitar, and I watched the entire thing happen. I jumped in my car and took off after them, but I lost them quickly.

It wasn't so much the loss of my guitar that bothered me, but the fact that it was common knowledge in the area that my house was the parsonage for the church, and these two guys if local, which they likely were, would easily know who I was. They knew I had watched them steal my guitar from the church, and they knew they had gotten away. As irrational as it may have been, I had anxiety for months that they would come to my house and do something. Maybe they'd wait until I wasn't home, and they'd come and harm Amanda. Or maybe they'd come in the middle of the night and attack us both. I lost sleep for weeks because of these two guys. I basically lived in public housing in Dassel.

I couldn't have been happier to have total privacy in Surprise. Amanda and I were also excited about new community. Surprise wasn't really anyone's hometown. Nearly everyone who lived there wasn't originally from there. This was actually true of much of the Phoenix metro. All I ever knew of Phoenix growing up was that it was the hottest city in the United States and that it was where people went to retire. With golf courses everywhere and plenty of sunshine, I could see why. I played golf a few times while living out there, and *I don't even care much* for the sport or the experience.

The church was a completely different change in lifestyle for me.

The campus was huge, with different buildings spread across the site representing the different ministries and services offered by the church. In the center of the site was the main building, which had the lobby and auditorium in the center. Around the parameters of the building were the preschool ministries, creative arts suites and offices, and main staff offices. I worked in the creative arts suites, mostly out of the green room, which was a space for the band to relax on Saturdays and Sundays during and between services. The green room was nicer than any place I had ever lived. It had a state of the art kitchen and living room, with better furniture than I had ever had in my life. Space for offices was a commodity as the church had grown fast and had to reclaim what were once offices for general space. For that reason, the church had given me an office in a storage closet upstairs. I never spent anytime in that windowless room, though. Instead, I sat at the dining room table of the green room during the work week.

Attached to the green room was the Worship Pastor's office. Jon had just come on staff and made hires, including me only a few months earlier. He and I couldn't have been more different. Jon represented everything I wasn't into about worship culture in the American church. He loved and adored Christian radio songs, and I can't listen to contemporary Christian music without feeling sick to my stomach. Jon also came into his career a generation before me and with that very much emulated the musical hero's of that era. Jon had played in some semi-successful regional alt-rock band in the early two thousands and with that had made his way into the church worship world as so many former Christian rock band guys do as their music faded into irrelevance. I'm not saying Jon was right or wrong or good or bad. He and I were just vastly different. Yet for this reason, I saw a potentially great strength. Where he seemed dated and irrelevant, I was fairly progressive and new. And where I lacked some age, wisdom, and experience, Jon had it. And as I understood it, that's why Jon had sought out to hire a couple of guys who were different than himself. I immediately respected Jon for this.

And with that goal, Jon had hired Ryan and me. I had come from the church in Minnesota, and Ryan from a church in Texas. Ryan and I were basically of the same age, both married, both without children, and both seeking great community. We became friends very quickly, mostly around our shared experience of trying to make sense of Jon and the rest of the worship department, for that matter. Up to this point, everywhere I had worked had been somewhat built by me, organically. We started small, and we grew. This was true when my ex and I were together and I was working in Harrisonburg at her home church. I had taken that church from piano and hymns on a Sunday to having modern music with a full band. Then in Charlotte, while I had inherited a band from the prior Worship Pastor, I was able to add many musicians quickly and shape it toward the vision I had, as unpolished as it was. Later in Dassel, I was given three guys who were a rhythm section of drums, electric guitar, and bass and with that grew a solid worship band and experience.

But here in Surprise, I wouldn't really be building anything. There was a well-established band and team already here that I had to assimilate into. I would lead the music with them at times, but my primary role in Surprise was at the back of the room on the sound board and then post-producing the music during the week. It was a very technical job. Jon could handle the weight of the department and church, and I could just keep my head down, put in my hours, and in my own time continue chasing my own music and creativity. Essentially, my work at the church in Surprise would pay the bills, but my career would be focused on building my personal platform, separate from the church. Ever since my first year in vocational ministry, I've always dreamed of what a normal nine-to-five job looked like. I had fantasied it and romanticized it. I had dreamt of having off time. I had created this entire scenario in the 2D shadow world, and with the move west, I had finally made it a 3D reality.

There's that classic saying that "the grass is always greener on the other side." We're all guilty of believing that at some point. With my first marriage, I was guilty of believing the grass would be greener on the other side of how awful our relationship was. With every job that I had worked in my career, I was guilty of always believing the grass would be greener on the other side. It's a tempting thought, but it's a regression into that shadow world. It's a distortion of reality and ratio-nality. It also borders breaking the law God designed for us to live by. I'll admit myself that the Ten Commandments read very ancient as they are, but if you look at each one logically and follow its conclu-sion, you'll see how beneficial they are for you and society. I think that believing the grass is always greener breaks one of the commandments and is a form of coveting. It's a form of envy and jealousy. It's not good for our hearts. Maybe it's not directly something that wanders far off of the path God has for us, but there is character in learning to be content, not always wanting what may be on the other side of the fence, or the other side of the country for that matter. The grass was not greener in Surprise because there wasn't even grass at all, just rocks. And things do not grow out of rocks.

There wasn't one particular moment that I can look back on as to when I realized I had made a mistake moving here. I imagine it was kind of like falling, but when you're in control of the fall, not an acci-dental slip like on the rock wall at the YMCA, but like a skydive. First there's the anxiety you feel before the jump. You know you made the decision to do this and be here. You knew what you were getting into. Next is the initial phase of the fall. Gravity pulls you. You accelerate. You feel the sensation in your stomach and all over your body. You're somewhat in shock. Then at some point, you hit terminal velocity, and the feeling of acceleration levels out and you can experience the fall without all of the chaos. Eventually, you'll pull the parachute and land safely on the ground. At least that's the idea.

The anxiety began during my first few weeks while I was figuring this place out. There was Jon, who I was quickly realizing that the strength I had seen of being vastly different was really just a source of frustration for both of us. Then there was the Lead Pastor, who, in my opinion, couldn't have been further from demonstrating a pastor's heart or character. He seemed very insecure and, honestly, mean. I watched him belittle a nineteen-year-old intern to the point of tears in front of a sixty-person staff meeting because a graphic wasn't exactly what he wanted. He called him stupid. I sat there in shock. This kid wanted to be in Creative Arts Ministry. Today he's an assistant manager at Starbucks. I'm not sure that he's stepped back into a church since he left this place.

I think it's generally unfair to point fingers at church leaders, especially those in the highest leadership positions. I'll be the first to admit I don't know everything about the situations I witnessed or pretend to not always believe there are two sides to every story. That said, I've been realizing as I've been in the church longer that it's ok to call out and see consequences of poor leadership. If we allow the church to be known internally or externally for scandals or corruption and we don't speak up, we're allowing the church to be injured.

Think about all of the scandals rocking the Catholic Church in the last several years. So many victims are coming forward sharing information that has been hidden and covered up for years and reliving great pain through it all. And unfortunately, it's not just the offenders on trial, but the reputation of the entire church and all of Christendom. In the evangelical world, I think about Mark Driscoll and Mars Hill. He was once one of the most influential pastors in the world, a common name in ministry. The church he led was a beacon and model of successful ministry. Yet he made poor decisions and hurt a lot of people. Then he didn't apologize or make things right fast enough. And now what I think of when I hear the name Mark Driscoll is very different. But it's not just Driscoll. There's Bill Hybels, who led the largest church in America at one point and birthed the vision of multisite churches that nearly every large church in the United States now embraces. Yet Hybels was involved in several scandals involving sexual misconduct. And when caught, he and his church shamed and attacked the women who were accusing him. Much of the staff of Willow Creek Community Church resigned immediately at this moment, including their Teaching Pastor Steve Carter, who wrote an open letter explaining why he was leaving. And it was clear. He had to call out the corruption and pain caused by Willow and Hybels and the unrepentant position that was taken.

I had even found out that the prior Lead Pastor of the church I was now working at in Surprise had been part of a major scandal, having an inappropriate relationship with a married woman he was counseling. Once this came to light, he had to step down, and the denomination sent in an interim Pastor to see the church through transition. That interim Pastor had spent a year at the church and recently transitioned as the new Lead Pastor. He had hired Jon a few months ago, who hired me. *None of this was disclosed to me while interviewing.* This is a traumatic story, with a lot of pain for this church. Things were not healthy here.

And from my observations, this new Lead Pastor of the church in Surprise was not a good man and certainly didn't exemplify qualities I'd want to see in Jesus or shepherd a flock of people to be like Jesus. Even in my first few weeks of watching how he led, I knew I was standing in a small aircraft with an open door, wind rushing across me. I had stepped up to the edge and looked down upon the earth. From up there, you can't see things clearly, only the outlines of roads and fields and forests. Now the question is, when would I jump? I knew I wasn't going to be landing with this plane.

As I debated about that jump, I also had to think through the anxiety I was feeling with the band and the worship team. Some of them were paid and treated the church's stage like any other weekend gig. Show up, play the songs, and immediately head out. There was very little healthy community. And some of the vocalists were major divas. There was one woman on the team who I gave feedback to after a rough set. I didn't realize the amount of drama I would be in for the next several weeks simply for telling her she was a little flat in the song she led. I was hired to oversee the audio experience of this church. I was hired to ensure that things went off with excellence, both in the moment and in the postproduction and mix. I had to tell her, and I told her with love. I encouraged her leadership, gave her the feedback, and then affirmed how gifted she was. This wasn't my first time giving someone feedback, and I know how sensitive musicians and artists can be.

Yet this lady literally went to the Worship Pastor and met with him for an hour about how awful I was. Then she did the same to the Lead Pastor, who already had been demonstrating he wasn't a fan of mine. I didn't realize that her husband was a local radiologist and that they were major financial supporters of the church. But should that even matter?

She even went to my personal website, downloaded some of my personal music, and began circulating my songs around the worship team, asking them if they thought I could sing or play guitar well, and overall just criticizing me as an artist. All of this simply because I had told her she was a little flat in a song and asked her to smile a little more to correct it. I had never in all of my years experienced something like this. At least she bought some of my songs on iTunes to make a point. I made a little money in the drama.

Anxiety reaches a climax right before the jump. They say your first jump is incredibly difficult. People freeze and lock up at the door. Then the instructor or guide has to push you out. My anxiety hit its climax with an email that showed up in the desert, near Yuma.

When I had interviewed, I had many things booked on my personal music calendar already. One of those things was a large conference in the Los Angeles area that Amanda and I would be leading worship at for a second year. I had given Jon my calendar while interviewing and gotten his affirmation that my personal gigs would be no problem if I came to work there. They had never been a problem in Dassel. In fact, the church in Dassel was always so excited for us to get those opportunities. Even in my first week in Surprise, I had printed out and emailed Jon my dates through the end of the year. Jon again affirmed me that there would be no problem. It was part of negotiating the job, and this freedom was one of the reasons I had moved to Surprise. It was one of my non-negotiables.

And in early July, it had come time for the gig in Los Angeles. We were going to San Diego first to meet up with another bandmate and then head to LA. One of our bandmates from Minnesota, James, flew down to play that gig with Amanda and me. We picked him up at the Phoenix airport and made the drive to California. We drove across southern Arizona, seeing the border fence and the sand dunes in the desert. The land was completely barren, the seclusion much like Wyoming. As we approached the halfway point of our drive near Yuma, my phone notified me of an email I had received from Jon. I quickly glanced at it while driving, and my anxiety peaked. In his email, Jon told me it *had been decided* that day by the Lead Pastor that I had abandoned the church by taking this time off, and that I needed to turn around and come back. I needed to forfeit the conference that had booked me a year prior or face the consequences when I returned.

I pulled over on the side of the desert road, surrounded only by sand and brush. I stepped out of the car, walked to the front, and leaned against the hood. I didn't say anything to Amanda or James initially, just asked them to give me a minute to process an email I had received. I had been at this church for only six months at this point, and I had honored everything I had been asked to do. I was present every single day, arriving early and staying late most days. I had accomplished every technical thing they asked for and had performed my job well. While I knew I was standing at the open door of the plane, I wasn't expecting to jump anytime soon. Yet this email became the guide who pushes or pulls you out. And he had grabbed me and pushed me out the open door and into the open sky with everything he had. Even the days before I left, I had double- and triple-checked with Jon to make sure all was well and things were covered. They were. I got back in the car after a few minutes and shared with Amanda and James what was going on. We all sat there in silence. I put the car back into drive and continued west.

THE WEST

C alifornia may be my favorite state in the nation. It's definitely the most diverse state I've ever been in. It's got it all: diverse people, diverse landscapes, and diverse thoughts, opinions, and perspectives. And it's huge. I first visited California many years ago when Amanda and I were booked to lead worship at this same conference in Anaheim. The conference flew us into LAX from Minneapolis, put us up in a beautiful hotel, gave us a driver, and took care of our every need while we were there. The moment I met the guy who booked us, he drove us to see the Pacific Ocean. He knew I had never been to California before and how much I wanted to see the Pacific. We walked out onto the soft white sand and over to the shoreline. We felt the cold water wash over our feet and ankles. Even though I had spent so much time at the beach growing up in eastern North Carolina, I had been landlocked for years in Minnesota. We were loving those moments experiencing California and walking along the Pacific for the first time.

Since that initial trip, we've been back in California several times. A few years ago, we drove the Pacific Coast Highway from Los Angeles all the way to Redwood National and State Parks, not far from the Oregon border. This is a dream drive. You go through big cities and small towns. We had driven from San Diego to Los Angeles before on the PCH and through all of the little and large beach communities. For this drive, we would start in Los Angeles and take the PCH north through Santa Barbara, Big Sur, and then into the Monterey Bay. We'd stay in Monterey and then visit Santa Cruz and onto Mavericks. We'd see San Francisco and cross the Golden Gate Bridge, then continue into the foggy and moody coastline of Northern California. We would stop in Trinidad and see the incredible and unique landscape of the oceanfront there, with a tiny mountain or giant boulder, however you want to describe it, sitting offshore in the ocean. Then we'd go into the Redwood National and State Parks.

As much as I love the entire state and coastline of California, there is nothing quite like Big Sur. The highway runs along the mountains and cliffs, overlooking the ocean nearly the entire time. There are no beach houses and no cities. It's just landscapes. It's rocks, sand, and water. For a moment you would believe yourself to be in northern Italy, winding along on the railway connecting the five villages of Cinque Terre. It's a similar view. Then you pull of at McWay Falls and suddenly it's as if you've come to Hawaii. And everywhere you go along Big Sur, the beachfront is as it's always been, with only the arched concrete bridges as evidence that man had developed something here. We drove across a bridge and around a bend and saw the rocks and sand covered in elephant seals, basking in the sunlight. Moments like this don't seem realistic for a drive in America. Everything is so new, so modern, and so developed. Seeing the bison in the Black Hills or seals along the beaches of Big Sur is a reminder of how open and untouched much of this nation actually is, with so much remaining to be pioneered and explored. So much is waiting for you and me to step into its beauty.

One of the greatest things about driving the PCH is that it's hard to compare and pick your favorite sites. As amazing as Big Sur is, the redwood forests of Northern California are also an incredible sight. There is nowhere else in the world to see naturally occurring redwood trees except on the west coast. To me, seeing the redwoods gave me the same feeling as seeing the Grand Canyon. Words cannot describe them. Sure they're just trees, but they're so grand and massive that they defy anything you have ever seen. When we stepped onto a path to hike through Redwoods National and State Parks, we felt like we stepped back into the young earth. We felt so small. The trees not only towered two to three hundred feet above us, but some were wider than any car or truck I've ever owned. In fact, we actually drove our rental car through one of the redwood trees. The longleaf pines of North Carolina that I grew up surrounded by were merely toothpicks to these monsters.

We once stopped along the PCH at one of the lowest elevations of the drive, where the highway descends like a carnival slide to the ocean. We pulled into a gravel lot, where a few cars were parked. Sitting on a rock was an old man playing an old acoustic guitar. On the man's head and his shoulders were bunnies. Yes, bunnies, living, breathing, and completely relaxed bunnies sitting on his head and his shoulders. He was all alone, having a Mary Poppins experience here in the coastal wilderness. I listened as he sang songs I had never heard, but I was so distracted by the bunnies. I was trying to figure this situation out. I wish I would have just asked him, but sometimes our imagination produces better, more inspirational reasons for the things we see and experience. I imagined he was a nomad, a supertramp. He was someone who wandered the country on foot, with his bunnies and without any cares. He was free. I imagined his life wasn't easy, but he could be wherever he wanted, experiencing whatever he wanted. And I imagined God was teaching him truths that can only be heard in the freedom of the wild—truths about minimalism, truths about the value of all living creatures, and truths about sonship and what it means to truly be loved.

Beautiful cities. Beautiful landscapes. California has it all. I had imagined the drive from Arizona to California to be a bit lighter, a bit more fun. We would catch up with James, and true to himself, he would goof off and have us laughing the entire drive. But Jon's email had made the drive heavy. At this point, I wasn't exactly sure what I was going to be coming home to. I didn't even know if I wanted to come home. Maybe we could just stay here in this amazing state. We could find a house, find jobs, and just make Los Angeles our town. Even today I still believe L.A. is my favorite city in America. People believe I'm crazy when I tell them that not even the traffic in L.A. bothers me. I was fine to just disregard the email Jon had sent me and never return to Surprise. But of course, that wasn't the reality.

I tried my best to focus on the conference that weekend, but it's hard to be present when your mind is preoccupied. In some of our free time, James and I rented surfboards and we drove down to San Onofre. James had never even seen the ocean, much less paddled out on a surfboard. My brother Daniel and I surfed throughout our childhood in North Carolina, and when I was in college, I kept that tradition up surfing in Corolla, not too far from my school. I had never paddled out into the Pacific, though. We drove our car out onto the State Park beach. We parked the car against the small cliffs above the sandy lot, and James and I put on our rented wet suits. I gave James a quick lesson on how to paddle, how to pop up, and how to turn the board into the wave to ride it. After a few minutes, we began the paddle out. There were several other surfers out there in the line. We paddled out and joined them.

Amanda sat on the shore at the car and just watched us and relaxed. We were both processing that email, not so much the content, as we weren't surprised that this email had come in the text and tone that it did. We were more processing what was going to happen because of it, not what they were going to do, but what we were going to do. In a lot of ways, there really wasn't a recovery from this. *Maybe* when I got back to the office on Monday, I'd receive an apology. Or maybe there could be an honest two-way conversation. Either of those scenarios seemed about as likely as James actually standing up on a wave as we were sitting out there waiting in the lineup. And James never got up.

Surfing is a pretty quiet sport. When you paddle out, you may be part of a large group of surfers, but everyone is mostly in their own space and just taking in their own experience. Daniel and I have surfed together our whole life, but I can't think of one time where we've had conversations while out on the water. In those quiet moments on the sea, I was like Amanda sitting quietly by herself on the shore, both independently thinking about everything, thinking about where we were and where we would go. We both felt the guilt that we had moved ourselves across the country for such a short time. We had left our predictable and safe life in Minnesota for this.

As I was there sitting on my board, a wave was forming, and I couldn't have been in a better position. I turned to face the shore, cliffs and beach in front of me. I began paddling as fast and as hard as I could toward the shore to get the momentum I needed to catch the wave. As the wave began to lift my body toward the sky, I pressed the board down into the face of the wave, extending my arms and pushing my body up above the board. First, I went to my left knee, my right foot on the board in front. I began to speed down the face of the wave. As I hit the bottom, I quickly placed my left foot on the back of the board, pressing down so fast and hard the nose of the board lifted above the bend where the wave meets the surface of the water. I leaned right, and the board turned right. And for what felt like minutes, I cruised along the shoreline, going nearly a hundred yards down the beach. If you're looking at the shore, San Onofre has a feature very few beaches have on their shore. There is a nuclear power plant right on the beach. I was cruising toward it. Rather than trying to do any maneuvering on the wave, I just stood there, gliding above the surface of the water. You have to understand that on the east coast, we don't really have long waves. On the east coast, it's a fast ride and then it's over. But here I had taken flight, and it felt like an international flight rather than a domestic flight.

When the ride ended, I stepped off the board almost in front of the nuclear power plant, and into knee-deep water. I had ridden the wave all the way to the shore. Rather than paddle back out, I felt like I got what I came there for. I had ridden a Pacific wave. I made the long walk carrying the eight-foot-six-long board back to Amanda. James came paddling in, surrendering to the fact that it wasn't going to happen for him today. The three of us sat there, watching the other surfers ride their waves up and down the shoreline.

Terminal velocity. I had stopped feeling the fall. Losing the job in Arizona didn't scare me. I wasn't afraid of what it would mean. I wasn't afraid of being a failure. To fail meant you had to try, and I don't know if I ever really tried. Don't get me wrong, I worked hard, but I certainly wasn't mission-minded for this church. I thought the Lead Pastor was pretty awful, and I didn't want to work for him. And Jon and I were so different that we just didn't click, either. I wasn't the right guy for them. But it was deeper than that. The truth is I wasn't in my calling, and since I wasn't in my calling, I didn't really care what happened with that job. I don't know if this is how I'd operate today, but I would never again put myself in a position where I wasn't in my calling.

There's a simple formula for figuring it out your calling. And I don't necessarily mean your spiritual calling, though I would affirm that I think a calling implies a destiny and design, and if you don't think you have a destiny and design, then I don't understand how you could ever feel a sense of fulfillment and purpose. Your calling *leads* you to your destiny and design. And that formula that allows you to find your calling is to identify your passions, talents, and burdens:

Your passions + your talents + your burdens = your calling.

Your passions are the things you *love*. I'm not talking about things you surface-level love, but the deepest love you can mine for. What are you really passionate about? What gets your blood moving and gets you out of bed in the morning? I answer these questions as deeply as possible. For instance, I'm passionate about embracing creativity.

What's a step deeper and into the why? For me, to be creative and to live creatively is what I really love. I want that for myself, and I want it for others. I want to write. I want to play and produce music. I want to take photos and develop film. These are my creative outlets. Even deeper, to be creative is really to be following in the heart of God. He created all things. Shared experiences bring people closer together. Soldiers who go into battle together can emerge as lifelong friends because of their shared experiences. Creativity is a shared experience with God. It's a shared experience with my Father. I am so passionate about embracing creativity because of what it does for me and in me.

Then you have your talents. Most of the time, your talents fuel your passions. If you don't have talents to fuel your passion, your passions can drive you to seek out a skill set. Skill set does not equal talent, but harnessed talent always produces a skill set. For example, Amanda is an incredibly talented musician. I can show her just about anything on any instrument, and within minutes, she can mimic what I'm doing and play it. Over the years, I've sat with her and played piano, accordion, bass, guitar, and mandolin. Yet today, if I handed her my mandolin, she wouldn't have a clue what to do with it. She has this great talent as a musician, but she's never harnessed it for more than a minute or two here or there. I'm always pushing her to harness that talent and turn it into something, but it's just not really her thing. Therefore, she doesn't have the skill set. But she's also an amazing artist and painter, and she has spent years harnessing this talent with countless hours working this craft through numerous paintings. And because of all of this, she has this skill set that has developed out of her talent.

I like to think I'm a talented creative as well. I of course will always keep harnessing and sharpening my talents, but when it comes to music or visual arts, I have a natural talent that makes it very natural for me to acquire the skill sets needed to live out my passions. Talent without passion will never be fueled, like Amanda with the mandolin. But talent with passion will be driven. This is why your calling must begin with a combination of passion and talent.

Finally, you have to know your burdens. What breaks your heart? All of our callings should contribute something to the world, and to your world. Without a burden and thus a contribution, you don't really have a purpose. For me, I have many burdens, which have branches like a river with many subsidiaries. I'm burdened for people to connect with God through the arts. I'm also burdened for the arts to be good and quality in the church. In the Renaissance, all of the great art was in the church. Nowadays the mainstream art of the church embarrasses mediocrity at best. I'm ashamed that the church is putting out these low-budget, poorly scripted, corny movies. I'm ashamed of the thrown-together clip art graphics, websites, digital and print media, marketing, and branding that are coming out of many churches. I'm ashamed of the Christian radio and the quality and artistry of music being played from it. A quick Internet search of the words "Christian radio" and "Becky" will open your mind to the Christian creative industry. Years ago Seth Tower Hurd, a former Christian radio industry insider, wrote a piece called "What Becky Didn't Want (Or a Short Account of the Brief Life of Christian Hit Radio)." You likely won't find it anywhere today, but I bought his e-book on Amazon years ago. He outlines who the industry is after, "Becky," who she is in her daily life, and what lengths the industry goes through to make music specifically for her. Michael Gungor explains this as well in his book *The Crowd, the Critic, and the Muse*. And if your target audience is a middle-aged, married, part-time career-driven white woman from the suburbs with two children, then you're never going to have art that takes any risks or pushes any envelopes. And real art requires risk, individuality, and sacrifice.

So I have many burdens, and many around art in the church. But it doesn't stop there. I'm also burdened to see people be at their full potential. I am burdened when someone is held back from being their best. It truly breaks my heart, especially when it's because of distortions, or fears, or insecurities. The talent I have connected to this burden is my ability to eloquently speak, not that I mean public speaking, but I'm fairly decent at conversing. I've been told I have a "silver tongue" and can word things in a way that I can communicate truth in love fairly easily. And the passion that drives this talent and this burden is wanting to see leaders raised up within the church, within careers, within homes, and within themselves.

I've just demonstrated two separate callings in my life:

1. Embracing creativity + various artistic formats + producing quality and unembarrassing art in the church = a calling to

influence arts in the church. And I've lived this out seventeen years at the moment by vocationally working in the arts within the church. Even today while I oversee much more than just the arts, I'm still very involved and very connected to the arts we produce, and I always will be. It's one of my life's callings.

2. Raising up leaders + eloquent speaking + seeing people at their full potential = a calling to have influential mentorships. I live this out through the staff that I lead. I feel a responsibility for them, to speak into their lives, to develop them, and to help them be at their best. I will let them stand on my shoulders, or I will hold up their arms. Whatever they need. Because this, too, is one of my life's callings.

While I was somewhat living out my passion for creativity at the church in Surprise, and I was able to use my talents there, I certainly wasn't able to live out my burden because I couldn't make any of the calls that would control the content that we produced. And if I'm honest, I am fairly embarrassed even today still after all of these years later by the things we put out. I nearly cringed every week at something we produced. And I couldn't control any of it. My voice wasn't asked for or considered because I wasn't the guy in charge. Like Tom had told me in Dassel, I liked to be in charge. And liking to be in charge was part of my calling. It's not driven by the need for power; I could care less about that. My calling *demanded* that I have a voice. If I couldn't have a voice, or at least be a contributor, it was hard for me to feel called to what I was doing.

And since I didn't feel called, what was I really losing? If they let me go, what were they really letting go of?

We got back from California, and the Lead Pastor and Jon asked to meet with me first thing in the next morning. I went into the office and sat across from the two of them. It felt like I was in a courtroom. The Lead Pastor was the judge, straight across from me staring me down as I stood at the podium to make my case. Jon was to the left in the jury box, remaining silent during the trial but ultimately was empowered to make a decision to fire me. In that brief meeting, I was told that I wasn't to build any platform for myself. If I was to remain on staff at this church, I wasn't to pursue any personal influence. My social media influence needed to stop. My personal album sales on my own website needed to stop. During this season, I was writing a series of blogs and devotions from the Book of Revelation, and they needed to stop. I wasn't to do any more conferences or any gigs where I was a featured worship leader. If I wanted to keep my job there, I needed to forfeit it all. I was told my only creative goal could be to grow *his* influence. And honestly, I'm not called to that. Some men are. I'm not.

I've always had good intuition and discernment. As I listened to the list of unrealistic demands upon me to keep my job, I realized how insecure this guy was—not Jon, who sat in silence, but the Lead Pastor—how threatened he was, and how hurt he must have been at some point in his life that he believed the only voices that could have any influence out of that church was his own and those whom reported to him that he directly oversaw. I had watched many people get fired from that church in my brief time there. Now it was my turn. And rather than get fired, I told him I thought it was best that I transition out. I offered to give them thirty days as not to leave them in a bind. They agreed, and I walked out. I called Amanda and told her what was going on. There really wasn't any heartache. I had hit terminal velocity already. We had no idea what we were going to do next and where we were going to land, but we trusted things would work out just fine.

I didn't last the thirty days, unfortunately. Hot off my resignation, they immediately called Ryan in and fired him. Same reasons. I then told the Lead Pastor that I saw so much insecurity in him and was sad for him. I told him he needed elders and accountability, something he didn't have. I told him the church only had one king, and that was King Jesus. And two days later, I was asked never to return. And I never did.

Four years later, I was having lunch with some friends and I got a call from a Phoenix area code. I answered it, and it was Jon. I hadn't seen him or spoken to him since I walked out of the church's doors and was asked to never return. After all these years, Jon apologized for how things went down and told me I had been right about things. The Lead Pastor had done some really crooked and messed up things, and there was going to be a major confrontation of him that evening. It was another Driscoll or another Hybels. I don't even know the details, and I didn't need to know. Jon said he likely was going to be fired that evening himself. And he was right. That evening, as the scandal broke, Jon was fired. And Jon went on to plant a new church and even jokingly felt out any interest I may have in being the Worship Pastor. I smiled at the irony and politely declined, and that was it.

After I walked out of that church, it was time to pull the parachute. Normally in a skydive, you would have planned a landing site and pulled your parachute as the site became clear. But soldiers jumping out of planes in the Second World War just went for it. They landed in fields, and farms, and even trees. They pulled their shoot and landed wherever they could. This jump I had made wasn't recreational. It was warfare. And it was time to have a victory.

The River & Tree

Since we knew we were going to be leaving Arizona soon, and with no solid plan, Amanda and I planned two trips that we could easily do while we still lived in the southwest. First was the Grand Canyon. We woke up early one morning and drove to the south rim. We parked the car and walked up to the edge for our first look. You've probably heard that pictures do not do it justice, and this is true. It is so vast, and so wide, and so deep. The colors are so rich, with variants of red and purple hues painting across the earth. Nothing about the landscape feels natural, yet you know the canyon's history from grade school. We drove along the southern rim, stopping at every pull-off, and overlook to see a different perspective of the canyon. We spent the entire day there in awe. Then we drove home.

The second trip we took was to Las Vegas. This was a bit further of a drive, but we wanted to see neon lights and casinos before we left this part of the country. We booked a room at the New York-New York Hotel and headed northwest. We drove through the desert, passing sandy fields covered in Joshua trees. I put U2 on our radio, so the entire experience felt right. We only stayed in Las Vegas for one night, and I think both Amanda and I were fine just going for that one night.

Casinos felt sad to us, not glamorous as they appeared in the movies. We walked around the streets and saw people so drunk they were sick. We saw pornography and strip club advertisements everywhere. We saw an old man walk by us with several young escorts hanging off his arm. None of my reactions were coming from a place of being judgmental or looking down on these people. I don't know anyone's situation, if they're happy or sad or fulfilled or empty. But I do know this—that the Las Vegas Strip is an illusion. It doesn't represent a sustainable life. And the best life you can live is one you can sustain: a life with peace and harmony, a life fulfilled, a life with calling, and a life with purpose. And what was the purpose of the move west? We hadn't been here long enough to even figure it out.

A week or so after the conference in California and right after I was asked never to return to that church, Amanda and I were lying in bed one night. Amanda suddenly felt a sharp pain in her lower abdomen. The pain intensified. In a moment she got up to try to go toward the bathroom and fell to the floor holding her lower abdomen. I rushed over and picked her up. I got her dressed and into the car, and we headed toward the hospital. On the way to the hospital, the pain began to subside. When we parked the car to go into the emergency room, the pain was all but gone, and only some tightness remained. Rather than go into the emergency room, we sat in the parking lot for a little bit to see if the pain continued to get any better. Thankfully, it did. We went home, and when we got home, Amanda started bleeding as if she had gotten her period.

What it ended up being, as far as we can guess today, was a cyst rupture related to Amanda's PCOS. Since this night several years ago, she's had several cyst ruptures over the years, and we now know what it looks like and what it feels like. But this was the first time this had happened. And we thought maybe she had somehow been pregnant and miscarried. We didn't believe ourselves to be pregnant, but that night as we tried to figure out what was going on, miscarriage seemed to fit the symptoms. We didn't know how it could be since we tried for two years straight in Minnesota, with one year on fertility medicines. And in the last couple of years, we were saving for adoption and not thinking about getting pregnant. But we thought in that moment that maybe a fluke had happen and she had gotten pregnant and then miscarried.

For the first time since we sat across from the doctor in Minnesota who told us we'd likely never have biological children, we felt hope.

Even though we were wrong and we can confidently say today that we were not pregnant and that it was *in fact* a cyst rupture, this newfound hope started us down a new path to explore. We had come to Arizona in part to adopt a child. At this point we had barely started that process, but we had identified some agencies and began gathering all of the information we needed to get started. With this new hope, we needed to see a doctor immediately and see what was going on. There was a doctor I had heard attended our church in Surprise, and I sought him out. In a church as large as the one we were at, there were many stories similar to ours, and as we heard stories of infertility, we heard about Dr. Sawyer. He was a local OB-GYN, and he had apparently been very helpful for women with PCOS. We called his office and set up an appointment. We saw him later that same week. It was a surreal experience.

When we arrived, we filled out a questionnaire. We wrote down some facts about our history, our years of no results, and the most recent pain and possible miscarriage. I felt like were writing a small book recapping our history to date. We did all of this sitting in his personal office, on a couch. We weren't in an examination room or anything, just in a comfortable office. He came in and took the packet we were working on. He sat down in the chair across from us and began reading the packet. We all sat there quietly for what felt like an hour. I watched him read page after page, lifting or furrowing his eyebrows as he read along. He'd tilt his head sideways as he read something of interest and then straighten back up. A few times he put his hand to his chin as if he was searching our story for its deeper meaning. When he finished, he closed the folder and looked at Amanda and me. He had a faint smile on his face, and pushing his glasses up his nose, he said the three words that changed our life.

"Ok, let's pray."

He walked over to us and put a hand on each of our shoulders. Then he prayed over us. He pleaded with God for a child for us. He told God we'd be amazing parents, which at this point I was peeking up at him because I know he didn't know us, and I wasn't sure where he was getting this from. I had just lost a job. I had nothing else concrete lined up yet. I didn't know where we were going to live in thirty days, much less how we were going to make our car and student loan payments. Yet he prayed over us like no one has ever prayed over us before. When he finished ten minutes later, he handed me three prescriptions and told me to get them filled for Amanda and have Amanda start taking them immediately. One was for Clomid, again. The other was for metformin, a medicine used to help regulate type 2 diabetes. The third was for progesterone, which was to help the uterus keep an egg if fertilized. This combination of medicines had proven effective in many women with PCOS, and he told us to call him when we had a positive pregnancy. Hope.

After surfing that wave in California at San Onofre, we went to the hotel we were staying in that evening. We ate dinner at a restaurant next door and then settled in for the night. After Amanda fell asleep, I hopped onto two websites that are known for church staffing. One is curated and ran by a group of professional headhunters in the church world. The other are just listings of what's out there, posted by individual churches. That night while Amanda was sleeping, I updated my resume and sent it to the headhunters. I was looking at Worship Pastor jobs and stumbled across one for a church in Charlottesville, Virginia, called The Point. I knew this city, as I used to stop in Charlottesville for gas every weekend when I would drive from my college in Elizabeth City to Harrisonburg. I sent them my resume as well.

During those weeks after leaving the church in Surprise and trying to figure out how to make Dr. Sawyer's prayers have legitimacy—that I would be a great father and provider—both the headhunters and The Point responded positively. I first interviewed with both of them from the rental home during our final countdown to having to move. The headhunters liked me so much they flew out to me and interviewed me right in Surprise. The Point was a small church that had planted three years earlier in Charlottesville, and this would be their first full-time Worship Pastor hire. They interviewed me over our computer cameras. And both interviews were going very well. The headhunters wanted to place me at a church in Virginia Beach, and The Point was in Charlottesville. So it was obvious that a door seemed to be opening in Virginia.

It's a strange feeling to feel peace in uncertainty, to feel rested when all around things are moving fast in the wrong direction. I had spent most of this year beginning in the north and now in the west writing and recording songs inspired by the Book of Revelation. While there is much debate about this strange book in the Bible, I saw story and inspiration that I wanted to share with those who loved my music. I had successfully raised the money I needed to make this project a reality through Kickstarter, a platform for artists and creatives to fundraise.

And I spent my time in the west perfecting this project and recording it. At the end of Revelation is the vision of the River and Tree of Life, a vision of peace and rest. With this last year of transitions and uncertainty, I was able to write about peace and rest:

"The angel now has shown that flowing from the throne
A river runs through the city
Bright as a star, flows to where we are
Bringing endless life to the many
Can you see it now?
Come and sit by the river
Come and drink of the water
Come and share in the peace of God
And rest your weary head
The tree is bearing fruit for God to give to you
It will heal the pain you've been feeling
Its season never ends, its branches never bend
Its purpose is to give a new beginning
Can you feel it now?
We will see His face
We will bear his name
We will stand in light and we will feel no shame
We will bless the Lord
We will rule the day
We will stand in victory and He will light the way
We will sit by the river
We will drink of the water
We will share in the peace of God
And rest our weary heads"

We contacted a moving company, and with no destination or address, and a very limited budget, we figured out what we would keep and move and what we would garage sale. We ended up only keeping about twenty-percent of what we owned. We had a two-day garage sale the next weekend, the weekend before we moved out, and sold everything we had placed for sale. Literally, everything. We made thousands of dollars. I couldn't believe it. Thousands. This would help us get to wherever we were going and help us get established somewhere. We had no idea yet, but we knew we needed to go visit these two churches in Virginia. The moving company picked up our items to move to their storage warehouse until we had an address for them, and we filled up the car with what we'd need for the foreseeable future. And with everything secured and absolutely no plan yet, we were heading east toward some landing point on the ground in Virginia.

And once again we were on the road. We were searching for a place to call home. We were trying to identify that sweet bull's-eye on the ground to land. I knew that God had given me a purpose and had made me with a calling on my life. And he had used this time in the west to prepare me for what was next. I knew who I was. I knew who I didn't want to be. And most importantly, Amanda and I had hope for a family. If we were to have biological children of our own, their story would begin with our time in the west. Like generations a hundred years ago, their father came to the Wild West for new opportunities and a better life. As dangerous as the Wild West was for our hearts, we had survived it. We had shared in the peace of God, and we found rest for our weary heads.

THE EAST

There are times in your life when the right thing to do is to move on and not look back. In one of the earliest Bible stories, Lot's wife was told to move on and not look back. God was destroying the city they lived in due to their wickedness and corruption, and since Lot and his wife were righteous people, they had been spared. Yet as they fled the city, she looked back and immediately turned into a pillar of salt. Pretty hardcore story. Sometimes the God of the Old Testament is hard to square up with. Yet, it was a different time and different season of mankind. Literal. Figurative. Symbolic. Who knows. I was raised in the tradition of literalism and that the Bible is infallibly God's Word. I will one hundred percent affirm today that I believe the Bible is infallible and is God's Word. And I don't know if it's all literal, but I do know it's all true.

There is a philosophical depth to life that many never tap into. It's there, but we just go through life unaware of it, like the difference between "literal" and "truth." Literal is "as I say." Truth is "as I am." Truth is much greater than literal. There is so much lost when we try to make the Bible literal. There are definitely literal things, but even Solomon spoke of truths that weren't literal. An example is the Proverb to "spare the rod, spoil the child." Solomon isn't literally saying that if you do not physically discipline your child, he or she will be spoiled. We know that in our society today, many families raise their children without physical discipline and punishment. And their children are capable of being raised without being spoiled because parenting is a unique experience that requires unique strategies for every child. So what is the truth, then? It's that a lack of discipline will create a spoiled child.

I had literally left the east coast after my ex and I had split up. I had literally lived away from the east coast for years. Yet in truth, I was still there in many ways. I had family living back out east. I had pain still packaged up back east, collecting dust in an unresolved corner of my heart. I had dreams I left back east, not necessarily dreams for the east coast, but dreams I had abandoned because I thought I'd never see the opportunity for them to become reality. As I turned onto I-40 from I-77 in Statesville, North Carolina, on the day I left Charlotte for Colorado, I had thrown a middle finger up to the rearview mirror facing east to the life I had felt so ruined by, and I headed west never to return. And I intended to keep that vow. Yet here I was, sitting in my driveway with a car packed completely full with all we would need for the foreseeable future, ready to do the same, driving back east. I had moved on and not looked back all those years ago, yet now my headlights were illuminating the way back. And I didn't turn into a pillar of salt.

Two churches had invited me to come visit them and consider working for them. There was the church in Virginia Beach, which was large and near my brother. He and his wife had just shared that they were pregnant the week we were loading our car and that they were expecting in May. It was one of the hardest phone calls we had ever experienced. We couldn't be happier for them, yet we were watching something we had seen many times: another pregnancy. It was a reminder that we weren't going to have our own biological children. Though we had recently been given some hope, their phone call hit us really hard with the reminder that after being married and trying for children for over three years, we had nothing to show for it. My little niece or nephew would be coming in May, and I didn't even know where we were going to be living. And as hard as the phone call was, we put on the most excited and happy faces we could until we hung up. Then I held Amanda as she cried for an hour afterward.

Would Virginia Beach be a good place to call home? It was near the ocean, something I knew growing up. It was near my brother, something else that I knew growing up. It was going to be near the new baby, something Amanda and I would be excited about. And it was a great church, with great career potential for me. When I was in college only about an hour south of Virginia Beach, several of us would often come up the tidewater area to go to a mall, or go to restaurants, or go to the beach. But I hated coming to Virginia Beach back then. It was always overcrowded. It seemed rundown. It's expensive. *Surfer* magazine called it "a large liquor store with a zip code." And I knew a lot of people from my college who lived in the area, and I was sure of their opinion of me. I was sure they believed I was unworthy of the church and God since I had been divorced. Some of the more legalistic people I knew from college had slammed my Facebook inbox many years ago for getting divorced as if I had committed a sin so great that no redemption would ever be possible. For a while I even believed that. I never wanted to return to that feeling.

Then there was this other church, located in Charlottesville. It was a few hours inland from Virginia Beach, at the foothills of the

Virginia mountains. They were a fairly new church, only three years old. They were portable, meeting in a high school every week. I had never done that. I knew people who worked in a portable church and what it required of them week after week after week. I had gotten to know The Point somewhat over several weeks and was excited to come and visit. Charlottesville was a city I enjoyed passing through. When I was in college, I would drive nearly every weekend from Elizabeth City, North Carolina, to Harrisonburg, Virginia. I worked weekends for a church there, my ex's home church, and we'd leave after classes on Friday for the five-hour drive. On Sundays after church, we'd return back to our college just in time to crash for the night. Then there were classes Monday through Friday. Looking back, I have no idea how I did this for two years. We had a friend named Amanda who periodically would ride with us, and she was from Charlottesville. We'd get off the interstate at the second of the four Charlottesville exits and take her to her home. The first exit in Charlottesville was always my place to stop for gas on the way to Harrisonburg every weekend. I knew that view from Pantops Mountain very well, and the idea of Charlottesville as a place to call home was very intriguing.

Aside from the two churches, all of our relatives were back east. My mom and family had moved back to North Carolina from Colorado while we were living in Minnesota. My brother had settled in Virginia Beach. Amanda's relatives were in Charlotte. Grandparents, cousins, and all of the others we aren't close to were all back east. I've heard my dad say many times that "there's a thing as *too much* family." I had lived that statement as gospel truth. Amanda and I spent years away from everyone, and we thrived in it. The thought of moving back and being close to our relatives wasn't all that exciting. And the truth is that nearly everyone feels some responsibility to their relatives.

I'm a big believer in family. Yet I don't consider family to mean "related." I believe you've got *family*, and you've got *relatives*. Family begins with a choice. At some point, two people chose to be together and create a family. Amanda and I chose one another. She took my last name. She is my family. While I've got many relatives who share my name, I don't consider them all family. And I've got a lot of family that don't have my name. The church is called a family of God. If all Christians are sons and daughters of God, then we're all unrelated family. And we make that choice to be family. It wasn't forced upon us. It's ours to define. I've seen so many unhealthy people remain unhealthy because they're surrounded by unhealthy relatives that they label as their family. One of the healthiest things we did early on in our marriage was to "define the line," our threshold of tolerance until someone in our lives crossed the line. If that line was crossed, we'd simply close the door on them until they stepped back over the line. That line had simple parameters, and we've reinforced it for a decade with people in our lives, whether relatives, friends, church members, or anyone else. Our relatives were notorious line crossers.

First, we determined that we weren't going to be *deceived*. People that deceive us aren't building anything of value between us. Deception destroys trust, and trust is the foundation of any relationship. So people who lie to us and deceive us constantly don't have a place in our lives.

We also determined that we were not going to tolerate *abuse*. We weren't going to be verbally assaulted by the people in our lives. Amanda and I are both very peaceful people, and we aren't going to surround ourselves with people who are aggressive and lash out at us. There will always be conflict and disagreements, but no one should be abused or disrespected in them. This is true of sarcasm just as much as aggression. And we aren't going to tolerate it.

Finally, we were not going to make decisions based upon *guilt*. Plainly put, we were not going to be guilted. I came from an Italian family that spoke three languages: Italian, English, and Guilt. And I had made many decisions throughout my life motivated by guilt. Those days were over. When there was something to decide or discuss, we weren't going to be pressured into anything through guilt. We would make decisions based on what's best for our family and what would be most rational for us.

Deception, abuse, and guilt—all these things are potentially waiting for us to face back east, back near our relatives.

I've learned that it's somewhat normal to feel dichotomies like this, to feel like life is a paradox. On one side I had the unresolved tensions back east around the prior life I had left there, as well as the nearness of our relatives. All of this felt tense and uncomfortable. Yet at the same time, it was clear God was moving us back east, and there was excitement and anticipation for where we were going and where we were going to end up. We didn't know if it was Virginia Beach, Charlottesville, or maybe even somewhere else for that matter, even back out west. Maybe this drive and journey back east was for me to finally confront the last bit of pain and shame that remained in me from the years prior. But whatever it was, we were at peace.

Sunrise in Arizona felt like it came late the morning we left. We had sold almost all we had. All that remained was in a moving truck, headed to a storage unit in Las Vegas until we had place to move it to. And the things we needed for the foreseeable future were packed into our car. We had spent the last night in our rental home as campers, with blankets and pillows on the floor of the living room in this empty house. I could see where our couches sat, where our television was only a few days ago. Now they were all in someone else's home. I could see where my friends sat, as we played FIFA together and I always lost. In the front guest room, I remember hosting a couple from Scotland who were CouchSurfing through our city and reached out looking for a night. Then they tried to stay forever and I had to kick them out. And the office in the house was my studio, and in that studio, I had worked on my Revelation album for many hours. Every room in this house had memories though we had only lived here a short time.

With the anticipation for the drive and the lack of quality sleep on the floor, we were up before the sun. We did our final load out as the sun came up and made a place for Crunchy to explore in the back half of the car. We put him in to let him start wandering around the car, and we walked back inside to say our goodbyes to the house. We looked around, making sure we didn't forget anything, and when the house looked exactly as empty as it was the day we moved in, we walked out of the garage and pushed the button to close it one last time. We both sat in the car, looked at each other, and knew that with this new day, a new chapter of our story was beginning.

INTERSTATE 40

There wasn't a huge rush on our end to get to Virginia. We had a week to make the nearly twenty-five-hundred-mile drive. That morning as we pulled out of Surprise, we started by heading north to Sedona. Sedona is an odd place in America. Mystics believe there are natural vortexes there that can bring about healing, both physically and metaphysically. There are beliefs that the red rocks of Sedona emit a power that is unique to this place and has it origins somewhere deep in the cosmic universe, and with that power comes a renewal of your body, senses, and spirit. People come from all over the world to experience the phenomenon of Sedona. I think it's almost comical the way people will grab at anything spiritual. The longing for connection to the spiritual is the most oppressed part of our being. We shout "reason and logic" from all corners of society, and any mention of a spiritual longing will raise an eyebrow. Yet it's there, within us. People just don't discuss their faith in the same way they don't discuss their politics. Even some of the most devout Christians and evangelicals will keep their mouths closed about their faith out of fear of rejection, fear of shame, or fear of persecution. Yet it's perfectly acceptable to sit in a vortex in Sedona. What is wrong with us?

Amanda and I didn't go to Sedona for the vortexes, but to see the beauty of its red rocks. The vibrant green plants against the bright red rocks are the desert's version of the holly and ivy at Christmas. It's Santa's workshop in the western wilderness. Rather than elusive elves running around, there are ringtail cats that can be spotted if you're patient and quiet. We didn't get to spend too much time in Sedona, as we were just passing through. Just like how fast Christmas comes and goes, Sedona was over in the blink of an eye. It was only midmorning when we arrived, and we had many hours ahead of us for the rest of the day and a long way to go.

Soon after Sedona, we came into the Flagstaff area of Arizona. People don't realize how diverse of a state Arizona actually is. Yes, there are deserts with brown and red desert landscapes. Yes, there is the Grand Canyon, one of the wonders of the world. There's Phoenix, in the Valley of the Sun, a scorched earth city with giant saguaro cactus on the outskirts of town. Then there's Flagstaff, a city and region that seems to have more in common with Denver than Phoenix. In the backdrop of the city are snowcapped mountains, and the area is covered by alpine trees of more than a million acres of the Coconino National Forest. We weren't planning to spend any real time in Flagstaff, only stopping there for lunch. I wish we had known about this area a little more when we lived in Surprise. We had spent most of our time in Surprise exploring the White Tank Mountains, small desert hills right outside of town. I would have driven to Sedona and Flagstaff every weekend if I had known how beautiful they were.

We had driven north from Phoenix to Flagstaff. And now it was time to turn east. Growing up with divorced parents, my mother would take my brother and me from her home in Wilmington to see our father on some weekends. We'd see the same curious sign as we were leaving town. It read, "Barstow, California, 2,554." From our coastal North Carolina town, we'd see a sign identifying the other end of Interstate 40 in California, over two thousand miles away. And here I was, taking the exit from I-17 onto I-40 in Flagstaff. It's amazing when you think of how connected our country really is. From Flagstaff, I could drive all the way to Wilmington without making any turns. Twenty-two hundred miles of straight driving. From Flagstaff, I could pull into my mother's driveway only making a single left turn once in Wilmington, followed by a right turn onto her street. From 1956 to 1992, travel was revolutionized as our interstate system was built. My entire story has been made possible because of the interstate system. Without the simplicity of the interstate, there likely wouldn't have been a Colorado part of my story, or a Wyoming or South Dakota. There wouldn't have been a Minnesota or an Arizona season of my life. And just like a nationwide road trip that takes you from your home and brings you back, I had begun the journey back home when I turned onto I-40.

Many people don't realize that I-40 includes a large section of the historic Route 66. At least, it runs along this forgotten and nostalgic highway. Much of our drive was going to be right beside Route 66. I had driven the bulk of this many years before with my mother and brother when they had saved me in Russellville, Arkansas. We had driven west across Oklahoma and the panhandle of Texas right along Route 66 before turning north to Colorado. Now here I was all of these years later driving east on this same road. When I had driven from Colorado back to North Carolina before moving north, I had driven a different interstate. And here I was today, with four tires on the pavement of the same road where I broke down in the PT Cruiser. This drive was going to take me past many of the same landmarks I last drove by when I was a lost, hopeless, and abandoned young man.

One of my favorite songwriters released a concept album years ago called *Leonard the Lonely Astronaut*. The story is set in the distant future, and our hero Leonard is on a lonely mission. Leonard's story was that his marriage was failing and he was getting divorced, and during this tragedy his wife unexpectedly passed away. Heartbroken and guilt-ridden, he accepts a job as the only pilot of a space freighter on a cargo delivery mission to the edges of outer space. Due to the laws of relativity, Leonard would return to the earth in his lifetime yet with the earth significantly older. All of his friends would have grown old and died by the time he finally comes home. Leonard accepts this mission for the solitude and to return to a new earth. It's his escape. The author of this project is Andrew Osenga, and he even built a spaceship in a warehouse and converted it into a studio, making the entire album in this space. He even wore a custom-made space suit to record in. That's dedication to a project. This record had resonated deeply with me. As we turned onto I-40, it felt appropriate to listen to "Leonard." In many ways, the return east felt like I was coming home to a new earth. Osenga writes in the opening song, "Brushstroke:"

> I still sort of have a couple friends who told me I should change
> my plans and stick around
> But I buckled my seatbelt and knew how the fly felt
> with the windows rolled down
> I'll make some new friends, maybe with their grandkids
> That old crew will be dead but I'll be
> the same old, good-looking, miserable Lee
> I just wish that you could be here with me

I hadn't been far enough away up north or west for the theory of relativity to kill off everyone I knew back east, but I was at least hoping the pain of the past had been laid to rest—not just my pain, but the pain I caused many people who were in my life back then. As much as I felt alone and abandoned through the divorce, I had also abandoned all of my friends by running into isolation. The world is much smaller than we think it is. I knew even by being in Virginia I would see people from my prior life before I blasted off into outer space. It was unavoidable. The difference between myself and Leonard was that I wasn't "the same old, good-looking, miserable Lee," although ironically Lee *is* my middle name. I had been healed, renewed, and restored. East represents newness. It's a sunrise of a new day. It's a fresh start. It's light.

We had a goal to make it from Flagstaff to Albuquerque before stopping for the night. The sun set as we were starting our approach to Albuquerque. On the dark and distant eastern horizon was a major thunderstorm, yet there wasn't a cloud near us. We were driving under stars, watching lightning illuminate the sky. We watched the flashes of light crawl across the clouds and horizon like water running down a mountain. We never heard the thunder or felt the rain, but we saw the white light flash in the sky, reflecting off of the city of Albuquerque as we drove in. We didn't make hotel arrangements for any of this drive because we didn't know where we'd be every night. We had a plan and goals, but we also knew that there was a lot of uncertainty on a two thousand-mile drive. We hoped to make it four or five hundred miles a day, but we didn't know how we would feel after a few days of that. We gave ourselves some flexibility and freedom on this drive since we had the time. We pulled up to a hotel on the west side of Albuquerque and got a cheap room for the night and, with that, completed day one of the journey east.

The next morning, we grabbed a quick breakfast in Albuquerque and got back on the road. The sky was completely clear and sunny. They say Montana is "big sky country." I don't disagree. But so is New Mexico, the Texas panhandle, and Oklahoma. Open fields and three hundred and sixty degrees of horizon. The landscape doesn't change much for these ten to fifteen hours of driving. It's the same thing, on repeat. When I was in middle school, I used to always listen to music as I went to bed. I had a small CD boom box, and it sat on my dresser. Back then, I only had the music my mother allowed me to have, and it was all contemporary Christian music. One night I placed a Michael W. Smith CD in the player, hit play on track four because it was the slowest and softest song on the album, and got into bed. The song "I Will Be Here for You" started playing, and I laid in bed trying to fall asleep. It was wintertime, very cold in our house, and I had gotten warm under my blankets. Once the song ended, it started again. I thought maybe the CD had skipped or glitched, as scratched CDs were prone to do. Then the song ended and started again. And again. And again. Somehow, I must had hit the repeat button on the boom box when I started the song, and this song was going to be the only track playing on this night. I was too warm and comfortable to get out of bed and fix it. I just figured I'd be ok with it, and I'd eventually fall asleep.

Well, after about the seventh or eighth time hearing Smith sing that chorus, I couldn't take it anymore. I forced myself out of bed and just turned the whole thing off. It took a little while to get warm again and to fall asleep, but at least the repetition was over.

Not the case driving across these states: same fields, same bluffs, same grass, same gas stations lined up in a row, and same fast-food restaurants along the interstate. While we had the occasional Route 66 oddity to pick us up, we were getting pretty worn out on this drive.

When we arrived in Amarillo, we stopped at Rudy's Smokehouse for lunch. Texas is known for their brisket barbecue, and while Texans love to debate what brisket best represents their state, I am completely fine with Rudy's. I had experienced Rudy's years before in Austin, and I was excited to share this experience with Amanda. While we had lunch and took a break from the road, we looked at the map and discussed our plans. There were many ways to get to Virginia at this point, and not being in a rush, we decided we didn't need to drive it straight. Amanda had never been to St. Louis and wanted to see the famous Gateway Arch that stands with the city's skyscrapers. It's called the "gateway to the west," which geographically is kind of funny because it's really just the middle of the Midwest. Once you pass through St. Louis heading west, you still have to get across Missouri and Kansas before you get to the true west. The Gateway Arch is about as "gateway to the west" as the mountains of Tennessee, the cornfields of Indiana, or the airport in Tulsa. But we were going to drive up to it and see it. We needed a change of landscape.

For the most part, Crunchy was doing well in the car. He had moments where he wanted to lay on the dashboard or went a little stir-crazy in the back. But like us, he was just along for the ride. Amanda and I had begun posting pictures of him on Instagram using the hashtag #crunchyontheroad, and that kept us somewhat entertained. He was, after all, the third member of our family. And he had been through a lot of transition and change in his short life, too. It seemed like acceptance of change and transition was a cultural value of our family.

When I was a kid in the back seat of my family's car, I always imagined that the trees and land were the ones moving outside of the window. I remember the moment I realized it was *us* that was actually moving, not the land. I don't remember how old I was, or where we were, but I do remember the wow factor of that moment. But after driving across New Mexico and Texas, I thought maybe I had been wrong for most of my life. Maybe it was the land that was moving, not us. Like old cartoons or sitcoms where the background repeats over and over while the main characters drive, I thought I had been trapped in a loop. After what felt like forever in time but literally no progress, we finally arrived in Oklahoma City. For night two of this drive, we once again found a cheap hotel right off the interstate. Nowadays, we've raised our threshold for what we'll tolerate for a night. It was the hotel in Oklahoma City that did this for us. As we were loading into the hotel for the night, I stepped on a piece of broken glass. We actually found shards of broken glass around our room. We were basically told to deal with it. Thankfully, I wasn't cut, just annoyed. But since this night, we've stayed in better places.

It was time to head north. Rather than continuing on I-40, we turned toward St. Louis onto I-44. The change was exactly what we needed. We were now seeing trees, at least. We also were experiencing some variations in elevation. It's funny how small changes can be so stimulating. After a full day of driving through fields, the forests were refreshing. The trees created a mystery that began only twenty feet off the road, covering the land so thick we'd never know what was beyond the first few layers of trees.

Mystery can be magnificent. It can be marvelous. In the mystery, our imaginations get to solve problems and project experiences. The mystery genre is so fun because for an entire story, we're trying to solve the problem or case with the evidence that we see. And then there's the twist at the end, with all that we didn't see, explaining the whole story. I hope that when we reach the end of our lives, and we arrive before God, we can settle many of our personal life's mysteries. We know God has always been and will always be. He has no beginning and no end. One can conclude then that God is not bound by time. We are linear in time, with a beginning and an end, yet God is not. I think His foreknowledge plays into this as well. God knows all things because He can see all things because He can look at time as if it's on a plane rather than a line. I believe He sees time like we can see a dining room table. We can see all corners, all edges, and all points across the table. It's a plane, not a line. And I believe God looks at time on a plane. I hope that it's a spiritual state, not just for God, but all spirits. I like to believe that the eternal part of me, that part that is a spiritual being, will not be bound by time as well, that I will exist above the tabletop and will be able to look down on all of time. Then I can solve all of the mysteries. I can see all of the workings that were happening around me that I couldn't see in my linear life.

I think embracing mystery is healthy for us. In this life, it's ok to not know all things. We can't give a definite answer in every theological question, yet we can have faith. Where science or reason or logic or even apologetics fail to explain our views and positions, we rely on the mystery. We rely on faith. We rely on things being unexplainable. An immature person has anxiety in mystery. A mature person takes solace in it.

The mysteries of the Missouri roadside forests would be my entertainment. Occasionally I'd see a farm, or a house, or a car through the trees. And in my mind, I'd work out what was happening in the lives of those who worked, lived, or owned these things. And I remembered that each of them is the center of their own story, and they have great struggles and great pain and great victories and great joys. And they are deeply loved by God, just as I am. This mind-set could make you feel like you're not really that important or special. When you realize everyone is important and matters, then the truth is no one is important or matters. Yet that is the paradox and mystery of God. Everyone is important, and everyone truly matters.

We pulled into St. Louis long enough to see the Gateway Arch. We didn't stay long. We saw it towering over the Mississippi at sunset, and then we crossed the mighty river and into Illinois. Rather than stop in East St. Louis, named the most dangerous town in the United States, we let the metro shrink in our rearview mirror until we could no longer see any light in the sky emanating from the city. And true to our travel pattern this far, we found a roadside hotel for the night and got some rest. We were now on the east side of the Mississippi and were soon to be closing in on Virginia.

NASHVILLE

We were several days away from our scheduled meeting in Charlottesville, so we decided to stop and visit one of my favorite cities, Nashville. We left Mount Vernon, Illinois, for Nashville after breakfast and reveled in the fact that it was only going to be a three-hour drive or so. Our drives for the past few days had been nearly all day, so the thought of only a three-hour drive was a relief. While we were feeling great about it, Crunchy had had enough. The moment we loaded the car out of the hotel, he started crying in the back seat. I had never heard a cat cry. He was meowing and howling nonstop. He paced the car, front to back. He couldn't be calmed down. He was done with the car and done with this trip. And while it was only a three-hour drive, it may have been the longest part of our journey. I thought we were never going to make it. Our peaceful drive had been turned into a sad nightmare, with Crunchy having a full-on anxiety attack for three hours.

The Nashville skyline was beautiful as we entered midday, not because there's anything particularly exciting about its skyline, but because it meant we had arrived. I knew we'd be in a hotel within an hour, and I could get Crunchy out of the car. We had booked a nicer hotel suite to stay in for three nights while we were in Nashville, and all of us (Crunchy included) were looking forward to the break. Once we got around the city, we made it to our hotel and got checked in. And Crunchy could not have been happier. Amanda and I felt a sign of relief when he started exploring the hotel suite's living room and bedroom like it was his new home. No more meowing. No more crying. It was finally quiet.

Almost all of my heroes lived in Nashville. They were all middle-class musicians, writing songs and performing them to modest crowds. They sold enough tickets, albums, and merchandise to be full time. And many of them had sold songs to major artists as well. None of them were wealthy, but each of them was living their dream to make their creative passions their jobs. They were living their calling. Many of them made themselves accessible to their fans, too. Throughout the years of listening to singer-songwriters out of Nashville and going to their shows when they performed close by, I had come to meet and connect with several of the artists that I admired. I had been to the small and large venues, the house concerts, and even the online shows.

When I was in high school, one of the mother-approved bands I could listen to was a contemporary Christian band called "Burlap to Cashmere." They were an extremely talented group of musicians with a front man and songwriter who often wrote profoundly deep lyrics that even today I can not understand. Songs like "Chop Chop" made no sense and still makes no sense to me. Yet I loved this band, and listening to them is incredibly nostalgic for me. They broke up when I was in high school as well, only producing one album in their original fashion. Their singer and songwriter, Steven Delopoulos, went on to have a solo career. It was reminiscent of the "Burlap" sound but more folky and true to Steven. I had grabbed his solo album as soon as it came out when I was in college and knew every word even though I barely knew any of its meaning.

Steven Delopoulos came to town on a tour when I was living in Charlotte. I had gone to see him with a friend at a tiny venue called The Evening Muse. This wasn't a typical tour, with an opening act or two followed by a headliner. It was three Nashville-based singer-songwriters, and they were each sharing their songs one by one and playing along and singing with one another. At the time, I had never heard of the other two artists who were performing with him. There was Katie Herzig, a very well-established staple of Nashville. She has a unique voice and style, and you've likely heard her on national commercials even if you haven't heard her songs. Then there was Julie Lee, a veteran of Nashville and an accomplished songwriter. She is an incredible writer, even having one of her songs recorded by Alison Krauss. Together the three of them created a very magical night at The Evening Muse. My friend and I sat right up front and watched them share their songs over the course of a couple of hours. When the night was over, we met each of them and shared how great their show was.

The following night, they were performing in Greenville, South Carolina, only a few hours from Charlotte. We raved to our friends about how great of a show it was, and we got a group together to drive to Greenville and hear them a second time. On the drive down, there was a major accident on the interstate, and we ended up arriving a little late. Once the show was over, Steven sat down with our group of friends in the closed venue and gave us a private concert of the songs we missed. This is how down to earth these Nashville artists are.

And as much as I loved hearing Steven, I really made a connection with Julie. Her songs captivated me as if I were a moth drawn to a porch light. I was drawn in by her voice, her songs, and the odd tunings of her guitar. When she sang, the room was silent. Bartenders stopped serving. Everyone just listened and watched as she created a moment that seemed to pause time. She was so grateful that we had driven down and brought a group with us to their show to see it a second time, and I was just grateful for her artistry. We connected on Facebook, and over the next several years, I would send her songs I was working on, and she'd give me her feedback. When I was living in Minnesota, I drove down to Nashville with a group of guys for a songwriters' workshop. I reached out to Julie, and she met our group for dinner and spent the evening telling us stories of her time in Nashville. After dinner, she invited us to a house party at another artist's home, and before we knew it, we were at a party with many people I had heard of in this community. There was singer-songwriter Andy Gullahorn, author Ian Morgan Cron, and even former contemporary Christian artist Jennifer Knapp. We had an incredible experience, all because of Julie. At the house party, I had shared with Julie that one of my all-time favorite Nashville singer-songwriters was Robby Hecht. Thanks to Julie, later that night Robby called me and set up a time for us to grab coffee.

Things even got better the following night. She invited us to a songwriters' circle, and we got to have dinner and share songs with a group of well-established writers and performers. One of the most successful and influential writers of the genre was even there that night, Julie's good friend Sarah Siskind. Sarah had written songs performed by Randy Travis and Wynonna Judd. She's also a Grammy-nominated vocalist. She's even toured with Bon Iver, and Justin Vernon referred to her as a "true student of American music." I was honored and humbled to be sitting in a living room eating pizza with this company, all because of Julie.

As soon as Amanda and I arrived in Nashville and got Crunchy in the hotel, I texted Julie to let her know we were in town for a few days.

We immediately set up a time to get together. The following morning, Julie had us over for breakfast. We caught up and shared about the journey east that we were on. We shared where life had taken us since we last saw each other and talked about the future. When we shared that we were headed to our first stop in Charlottesville, Julie shared that Sarah Siskind and her husband lived outside of town in the mountains and annually hosted a festival there called "The Festy." Julie was soon going to be headed there herself, as she does every year to be part of the festival. She spoke highly of the area and told us that she hoped it worked out for us to be there. Our conversation then drifted, as it always does, to the music we were working on. I showed her some of the Revelation songs I had recorded, and she showed me a project she was working on. We traded songs for a few hours and then said our goodbyes. She gave Amanda and me a poster that had been illustrated for her upcoming record of a woman holding her baby looking across a field at a train. It honestly reminded me of Wyoming. At the bottom she wrote us a note that said "Keep on following that still, small voice."

That was our intent, and even today that remains our intent. We were following that still, small voice east to Virginia. We were following that still, small voice to becoming parents. We were following that still, small voice toward our calling. We were following that still, small voice into all of the mysteries that had been prepared for us.

VIRGINIA

I t was only going to be a day's drive to Charlottesville from Nashville. We were back on I-40 again, and eventually we turned onto I-81 and up into Virginia. As we passed through Tennessee's final flagship of Bristol, we felt a sense of accomplishment from the drive. Arizona to Virginia is no joke. America is big. And a cross-country drive is not for the faint of heart. But we had done it. We had made it.

A few hours later, we passed by Roanoke. Then a few hours after that, we approached Staunton, where I used to transition from I-64 to I-81 every weekend while making that five-hour drive from my college in North Carolina to the church in Harrisonburg, which is only thirty minutes north of Staunton. And right outside of Staunton is a small town called Verona, where my former wife and I had lived before we moved to Charlotte. That interchange where I-81 meets I-64 was a sight all too familiar. Every demon who tried to destroy me during the many years before this moment began circling my car like vultures to a lifeless body. One of the reasons vultures circle something dead so much before coming down to devour it is because they are waiting to smell death on the carcass before coming down to eat. They circle what appears to be dead, waiting for the smell as confirmation. Then they eat.

My mistakes could have killed me. So could all of my failures. The shame could have killed me, or regrets, or disappointments. I could have been killed by unmet expectations, or seeing corruption, or being corruption myself. Loneliness and abandonment could have ended me. But I had survived. My faith had survived. My hope had survived. I may have had the appearance of death at some points throughout the years, but when those demons circled me in my car that night looking for confirmation, they didn't find it. And in a stretch of interstate over Afton Mountain, my spirit moved like John the Baptist meeting Jesus in the womb. I was full of life.

Sometimes it takes facing your pain and your past head-on to see if you can really stand up to it. I had come to terms with so much in theory, but I didn't have to look directly at it like I would in Virginia, with so much of my personal history here. I didn't have to experience it while I lived across the country. I never had to be reminded of it. I could keep my distance from it and in the mystery or the 2D shadow world project a reality that things had resolved when maybe they hadn't. But to really stand up to your pain and your past, you have to look directly at it. I once had surgery on my middle finger after I broke it when playing intramural basketball in college. I didn't realize it was broken for six weeks, thinking I just had jammed it. When it never healed and seemed to be getting worse, I went to a doctor who immediately put me into surgery. He had to open my finger up, reset a chipped piece of the bone, and put a long pin in my finger all the way to my proximal interphalangeal joint, which is a fancy way of saying "middle knuckle." He then had to place a wire through the bone on the top and bottom of my finger to hold it in place. By the time a day or two went by, I had to remove the bandage to clean the surgery wound. I could barely look at it. It was so gross.

And that's how it is when we have to look at wounds of our past. We don't want to look at them. They're gross. It would have been better if my finger just healed on its own and in eight weeks or so, I could unwrap that bandage and all would be well. Instead, I literally looked at it and cleaned around the bloody mess daily for six weeks. I literally had to look at a metal pin sticking out of my finger every single day. Yet cleaning it and treating it daily is why it healed alright and why I have, for the most part, full use of that finger today. Of course there's a pretty gnarly scar, and my fingernail no longer grows the same, but it's healed. And everyday it got a little easier to remove the bandage and clean it. You get desensitized to it over time. Whether it's seeing a gross surgery wound or seeing a gross story in your past, the more you can look directly at it, the more you can deal with it.

My time in the wilderness, from Blessings Ranch to the Badlands, from Minnesota to Arizona, all made me look at my past, my story. I had spent these past years treating wounds. And when I came down the east side of Afton Mountains, there were no scabs to pick. Sure there were scars, but you can't pick open a scar. That's true healing.

We arrived in Charlottesville after dark and checked into the hotel that had been reserved for us. We'd be here through the weekend and then onto visit my brother in Virginia Beach. On the next weekend, we'd be at the church in Virginia Beach and then head to visit my mother until we got word of what was next. We were fairly certain that one of these two churches would offer me the job, but we weren't sure which one. We also had no backup plan, other than to see what would happen should neither work out. While a situation like this could carry a certain weight or pressure, I felt completely free to make the right decision. I didn't want to move anymore. I wanted to find a place for the long haul. And for that to happen, it had to be a right fit. It couldn't be a decision out of desperation or looking for greener grass.

The following morning, we began the interview process with The Point. First, we met the Operations Pastor who had been interviewing me for a couple of months. We had breakfast together at a local bagel shop and then spent the day sightseeing the city of Charlottesville. In the afternoon, I led their band through a time of rehearsal and preparation for Sunday. Later that night, we had dinner with the Senior Pastor and a few others. Everything seemed great, but I didn't know how in tune to myself I really was. It was a very long day, after many very long days of driving. It also may have been my guardedness, as I didn't want another Surprise. Literally.

We really enjoyed our time meeting these people who potentially would share life with us. We were hoping for a magic moment, that clear "yes" to be spoken from Heaven the way God's voice called out affirming Jesus's baptism, but God remained silent all day. I've come to realize that not everything in life comes with grandiose affirmation. Many of our decisions are just that, our decisions, just like we choose our family, the way I chose Amanda and she chose me. Yet in the right decision, there is great blessing and favor. And I wanted some of that. We could do this, or we could do something else. Whatever would be right. I tried to keep an open mind but also tried not to get my hopes up too much.

But that entire mind-set was quickly thrown out the window the following day. We arrived at the school where the church met every week. Setup began while it was still dark outside. The southern morning air was damp and thick, with an opera of insects singing out from the surrounding woods. This was the welcoming choir to the trailers of The Point. We participated and watched as dozens of people assembled the entire church out of boxes from three trailers parked outside. The stage and auditorium are all built out of boxes, the children's church all built out of boxes. Signage went up everywhere, both inside and outside. It was a tremendous amount of work. The church in Arizona

VIRGINIA

was nearly seven times the size of The Point, and it took a fraction of
the volunteer hours to pull off a Sunday service. There had to be something really special about this church in Charlottesville that this many
people would show up before the sun to transform this county-owned
building into a Kingdom-owned building for the day.

It wasn't even just the setup, but it was the entire day, with people everywhere, serving however they could. No one came through
the doors without a volunteer holding it open for them. Kids of all
ages were loved and cared for and had a fun experience planned for
them by the various volunteers in Kids Point. This was a very different
experience than the flannel graphs I had as a kid at that small church
in Warsaw. The service in the auditorium was done with total excellence. The band was well prepared and incredibly talented. So was the
Production Team. Pastor Gabe's message was thought out, creative,
and well rehearsed. He was preaching a series called "Family Matters,"
and I didn't know what to expect. At the church in Surprise, someone
would have come out on the stage as Steve Urkel to make an empty
point. I appreciated that Pastor Gabe was speaking with substance
about what really matters in family.

It was an incredible morning. After the two services had ended,
everyone began loading the church back up into boxes and onto the
trailers just as efficiently as they had unloaded them hours before. As
we were wrapping up the day, one of the older members of the church
came up to me and thanked me for leading the songs. He then handed
me a stack of twenties to "take Amanda to lunch." When I counted
it out, there was over a hundred dollars in that stack. We'd get many
lunches for that kind of money. And after the entire operation was
over, I sat down with Pastor Gabe as we talked ministry philosophy
and theology for three hours. I left feeling like we made a great connection, and after experiencing The Point, I wanted to give my life to

it. I now had my backup plan. Should nothing work out, we'd move to Charlottesville and find jobs in town and call The Point our home.

Feeling so full from the weekend in Charlottesville, we loaded the car and went to Virginia Beach, only three hours away. The following weekend, The Point was bringing in another candidate for the job, and I wouldn't hear anything until the week following that. I had an interview in Virginia Beach that same weekend, so it made sense for us to go visit Daniel and Rachel. They were early on in their pregnancy, and we were excited to see them and celebrate with them. We arrived at their house and got ourselves settled for the week. I was mentally preparing for the upcoming weekend interview, but I couldn't stop thinking about The Point. It consumed my thoughts from the time I woke up until I fell asleep. I was daydreaming of the things I'd want to do there and who I'd want to be. I was imagining the kind of leader I'd be if I was at The Point. And I liked what I was dreaming about.

One thing I've learned from moving so many times in my life is how critical it is to evaluate what's working for you and what isn't. Editing yourself is a blessing that only comes through relocation. With every move and every new community comes a chance to take a look at who you are and make changes. I had learned a lot about the kind of man and leader I wanted to be during my time in Minnesota. I may not have perfected that man, and honestly I still haven't, but that season gave me vision. Then in Arizona, I saw other leaders behave in ways I never wanted to be. My dad has said to me many times throughout my adult life that I had been shown "how not to live my life" by the way I grew up. I always understood that as an apology. Negative role models are just as valuable as positive role models. It's just as easy to identify who you don't want to be as it is to identify who you do want to be. I knew who I didn't want to be and what parts of myself needed some work, what needed some surgery.

So who do I want to be? I want to be *authentic*. I don't want to feel like I have to be someone I'm not. That meant I had to either be true to the man I am or become the man I show myself to be. Thankfully, I had failed for many years trying to become the man I showed myself to be. I had learned to be true to the man that I am. But that isn't a license or excuse to not be a good man. Contrary, I believe I am a good man. I constantly consider my motives in everything, as I believe motives are a true test of goodness. People don't always make the right decisions or do the right things, but I'd wage that most of the time, their decisions or actions are done with good intentions. I may be an optimist, but I believe people, at their core, are good. This is why if someone was to fall in the street, you'd see strangers run to them and help them, with no prior knowledge or strings attached. This is just innate within us. That's not true of just the south, or America, but true all over the world. No one teaches us to be this way. We just are, by design. I don't accept that people are selfish or evil by nature. I think this would contradict being made in the very image of God.

I want to be *wise*, which meant I have to think before I speak. I have to process things before I make a decision. I needed to lean into my discernment and speak the truth in love. The Bible says that if any-one lacks wisdom, ask for it. I did just that. I asked for wisdom. I still ask for wisdom because that's the kind of man I want to be.

And I want to be *influential*. I don't want that because I'm self-cen-tered or self-driven, rather I want that because I think I've got a story to tell and a victory and freedom I've found. I want to share that with those who need it. I've been thinking a lot about influence because at the end of the day, leadership is influence. As John Maxwell says, it's "nothing more, and nothing less." So what makes someone influential? There are six areas in my life that I've really been intentional about and worked on to grow my influence:

1. **Likability**—If you want to be influential, people have to like you. That means you can't be a jerk. You can't use people. You've got to be fun and enjoyable to be around. You've got to be life-giving.

2. **Credibility**—You've got to prove you know what you're talking about. You can get credibility by education or experience. You must go before someone and find the way so you can show them.

3. **Consistency**—You've got to be a person who delivers the same results. You can't be awesome one minute and mediocre the next. This isn't to say you won't always be awesome, but if you want to be influential, you better be consistent with who you are and what you produce.

4. **Longevity**—Influence happens when you have been somewhere long enough to speak into things. You've proven you're trustworthy, and you aren't just looking out for you because that isn't sustainable. Longevity demonstrates you're looking out for the whole organization, or the whole group, which gives you a right to speak into it.

5. **Advocacy**—Leaders are advocates for those they lead. Lately I've been really feeling that I can't lead someone I don't believe in. If I want to be influential, then I better be "for" and advocate for those I'm influencing. Leaders win, and when you make others win as a leader, you win.

6. **Dependability**—Jesus laid out two principles around this. First, you "let your yes be yes, and your no be no." Be a man or woman of your word. You give your word value, and stick to what you say. Next, Jesus has a parable where he teaches that someone who is faithful in the small thing can be trusted with

the big thing. If you want influence, you demonstrate you're dependable, and you prove that with the small things. Then the increase in your leadership and impact comes with the bigger things.

That's the kind of leader I want to be. You know who I didn't want to be? I didn't want to be a man who led from insecurity. I didn't want to be a man who led or motivated from or with fear. I didn't want to be a man who was unsure of who he is and therefore can't lead others. A man who can't lead himself somewhere certainly can't take others anywhere. I knew who I was, who I wanted to be, and who I didn't want to be. And it was time to make a very tough call.

On Wednesday, just three days after we left Charlottesville, I called the church in Virginia Beach and withdrew my candidacy. My mother and brother thought I had lost my mind. I had removed the second option. But when I dreamed of where I wanted to be, it was Charlottesville. It was The Point. And even if I got the job in Virginia Beach, I don't think that fact would have changed. I'd be sitting in my office wondering how things were going in Charlottesville. That wouldn't be fair to anyone. It certainly wouldn't have been authentic. And I wanted to be authentic. It may have seemed like withdrawing this option for our family lacked wisdom, and maybe it did. But it was a worldly wisdom, one that said to value and pursue security over service. I'd rather give my life to the right thing than the secure thing.

We left Daniel and Rachel's house near the end of the week and drove down to my mother's house in Wilmington. When we got there, we spent time catching up with my mom, stepdad, and my youngest brother. Amanda and I went walking on the beach on Sunday evening, wondering how things went at The Point with the other applicant.

Deep down I was hoping he was terrible in every way. Maybe he'd be a heretic, too. But honestly, I wanted them to have whatever was best for them. I just hoped it was me. Amanda and I took some photos together on the beach at sunset, thinking it would be our last night of uncertainty. Sometime between the sunrise and tomorrow's sunset, we'd have an answer. In our most uncertain hours, we snapped some pictures together to mark the end of an era.

The call came first thing in the morning. The Point called me and offered me the job. I accepted before they could even tell me the details, and within twenty-four hours, I was back in Charlottesville finding Amanda and me a place to live. I signed the lease on a small apartment near downtown, and by the end of the week, we were unloading our car into that apartment. I contacted the moving company to tell them the good news, that we finally had an address. You know how sometimes you feel rushed and you do things quickly without figuring out all of the details? I had done this in Arizona when we hired a moving company to relocate us. It never occurred to me that our items wouldn't show up the next day. In fact, it would be five weeks before our household items would make it to Charlottesville, five weeks of living in a completely empty apartment.

So that we didn't sleep on the floor, we bought a futon for our apartment. It was our couch during the day and our bed at night. We had a computer sitting on a box that was our television, and we'd spend our evenings watching Netflix on a small computer screen. To cook, someone loaned us some pots and pans. And our limited clothing selection would have to take us into fall. We were making it work. These were some of our best days. Since we had nothing in the apartment, we spent many evenings learning Charlottesville through downtown walks and driving around the area just to have something to do. We were loving this new home. The Point was everything I wanted it to be. It was never going to be easy, but nothing worth anything ever is.

I had spent years nomadically camping in the wild of America, from the highest elevation in Colorado to the complete extremes in climates of Minnesota and Arizona. America is a wild nation, open and empty in its majority, plenty of space to go explore and to go discover. There's also plenty of space to run away to. But all wanderers long for home, and deep down, many want to return. I was back in the company of relatives and family. I had left years ago, planning to never look back because I was afraid of the pain that would accompany looking. But I looked. And I still look. The tabernacle had become a temple. The temporary had become permanent. The homeless had found home.

There is a philosophical depth to life that many never tap into. It's there, but we just go through life unaware of it, like the difference between "literal" and "truth." We literally had moved our life all around the country, but the truth is we were never home. And now, we were truly home, literally in Charlottesville.

FATHER IN THE WILD

In the right decision, there is great blessing and favor. It's been many years since we decided to come home. Within thirty days of moving into that small apartment in Charlottesville, we were expecting. Nine months later, our son was born. Blessings. Favor. Dr. Sawyer's prayer over us in Arizona had become a reality only two months after he prayed it. It had been three years of us wanting our child so bad. And it happened so soon after moving here that we felt an absolute confirmation that this was where we were supposed to be.

Becoming a father was all I ever wanted. And it finally had happened. I started this project because I wanted him to know where he came from. I wanted him to one day understand that even when I recall my hardest days, I look back with so much gratitude for them. They brought him to me. Had my former wife and I stayed together, I would not have him today. I would not have the journey and all of its lessons to make me the man I am now. I'm not justifying or excusing divorce. I know God hates it, and it isn't part of His plan for humanity. No heartbreak or death is part of his plan. Yet I believe God, as He says in His word, makes all things work together for the good of those who love Him. And I love Him, and I'm so thankful and grateful for His blessings and favor. And my life is evidence that He does in fact work all things together.

Had I not moved to Colorado, I never would have experienced the deep healing my heart and spirit needed. My time there healed wounds much older and deeper than what caused the divorce. Had I not moved to Minnesota, I would have never grown as a leader to discover who I wanted to be. Had I not moved to Arizona, I would have never grown as a leader to discover who I never wanted to be. And had we not been in Arizona, we never would have met Dr. Sawyer. And without Dr. Sawyer, his prayer, and his treatment, there would be no little boy sleeping soundly upstairs as I wrap this project up tonight. I don't believe everything happens for a reason or that everything is part of a destiny. But I do believe that God makes destiny out of our decisions. And if we listen to what He's called us to do, He finds a way to lead us and guide our steps. He is the good shepherd. He knows us, and we can know Him.

In my experiences, I've seen God redeem things much bigger than we'd expect to see. We always love hearing a life change story or how God delivered someone from some dark place or path. And even when we hear that story, we're usually only hearing the direct impact God made in their lives. But what if God was redeeming things around that life as well? Those are stories that should be told, too. God redeemed my story, and in doing so, He also redeemed my family's story. My mother and stepfather split up a few years after I left Colorado, and in that season of separation, my stepfather gave his life to Jesus. There is no greater evidence I've seen of God's redemption and the power of the Holy Spirit than to see him today, a wonderful man and grandfather. He and my mother reconciled and today lead a nonprofit ministry helping others. My mother lived a hard life in an Italian household, and it took over fifty years for things to get a little easier and a little more fun. Today she's living a life doing what she loves—redeemed, both of them.

While my actual father and I still only see each other a couple of times a year, I can feel in my heart how God has redeemed my need for more than that. While I often wish this was different, the redemption has been an internal one. We talk as friends, we enjoy our time together, and he has been there when we've needed him to be. He was there when we were pursuing adoption, and he was there for the birth of his grandchildren. It may not be the father and son relationship some of my friends have, but that's ok. It's enough because God redeemed the need for more. So it's not just my story that has been redeemed, but the stories of my family around me.

I've been at The Point many years now. It hasn't always been easy, but I've stuck around long enough to see God do incredible things. Character is developed when we stick to things. And I've firsthand gotten to experience what God can develop in someone if they'll stick around. Everything I had experienced in the years leading up to this move was preparing me for the wonderful life I would experience here. Like Job who had lost so much only to regain it, God had returned my life tenfold to me. Honestly, it's a hundred-fold. I'm a daily recipient of God's blessings and favor.

I found my Father in the wild. It's been in nature and in the wilderness that I've experienced God. It's been on the run and on the road. It hasn't just been in the church services, though I believe God is always present in the church. For me though, my most spiritually deep moments have been in the wild. Sometimes that's been literally in the wilderness. That's where God likes to go, and that's where I like to find Him. In the earliest story in the Bible, God is walking around the garden. I like to think He's still this same God and can be found walking around His creation. He's at the summit of Red Nose. He's in the Badlands. He's in Yellowstone. He's in the farmlands. He's in the desert and along the coastline of California. He walks through the Redwoods and laughs at those standing in the vortexes of Sedona. He is in the wild.

And then there are times when I've found Him in an emotional or spiritual wilderness. The Psalmist says that He is close to the brokenhearted and saves those crushed in spirit. So He's in the pain of a divorce. He's in shame and embarrassment. He's in loneliness and abandonment. He's in an absent or dysfunctional family. He's in job loss. He's in uncertainty. He's in death and grief. He's there in the wild, in your wild.

A few years after our son was born, we were expecting again, this time with a little girl and this time with no fertility treatments or plan, completely a surprise. Today I have two beautiful and healthy children. Blessings and favor.

And I've realized that I, too, am a father in the wild, not just to my children, but to those who I have led or lead. This is not to say that to them I'm a father, but I want to love and lead those whom God has put in my life as a father would. I have spiritual sons and daughters. While God's wild is in order, mine is chaos. My wild represents all of the unknown. It's a backpacking adventure, where I'm carrying limited knowledge and gear to parent and lead with. Sometimes I lack the things I need, but I find a way to make things work. It's like rubbing two sticks together to make a fire. I show up for my children. I always will.

One thing I want for my family is that they turn out better than me. I want that for Elijah. I want that for Marcella. I want that for anyone that looks to me as a leader. As much as I want to, I cannot spare them pain. They're going to experience loss, heartbreak, shame, disappointment, and everything else that hurts in this life. We all have a choice to make when we face these inevitable enemies, and I hope they chose paths better than I did when I was at my lowest, paths not just in their lives literally, but in the truth in their hearts as well. I hope they guard their hearts better than me. I hope they protect their reputations better than me. I hope they love and lead better than me.

I've shared several songs that have been written out of the different seasons of life I've experienced. While all of my songs are important to me and my creative legacy, nothing is as important to me as this song. I wrote it after Elijah was born. It's a truth from me, a father in the wild, for my children:

"I was laughing when I first saw your face
Overwhelming, a brown-eyed hurricane
Everybody's got a dream,
everybody's got something they're dreaming of
You are my victory, you are my destiny, what I gained from love
Every wish came true when I first saw you
I would give up everything if you would be better than me
It won't take much, just a bit more love and a little more honesty
And when you stumble, I'll help you stand up better than me
Keep your heart humble, be fast to forgive and slow to disagree
See it won't take much to be better than me
I was smiling when you said "I love you"
It took me back to when your momma said "I do"
Now I see what we've made,
and boy I wouldn't trade a single minute
Because every second counts,

and boy my heart would drought if you weren't in it
Changed with just a glance, you're my second chance
I would give up everything if you would be better than me
It won't take much, just a bit more love and a little more honesty
And when you stumble, I'll help you stand up better than me
Keep your heart humble, be fast to forgive and slow to disagree
See it won't take much to be better than me
There's nothing you can't do
Believe me when I say this to you
You can be anything
Better than me"

And where there was hate and all of its ugliness, there is love. Things I used to hate within myself or around my life have been replaced with love, acceptance, and even anticipation. Things I used to hate, I don't hate anymore. There is love. There is peace. There is redemption.

References

1. Lyrics from the title of "Here in America" is a song by Rich Mullins, from the album Here in America released in 1993, p. 38.

2. "But if they cannot exercise self-control, they should marry. For it is better to marry than to burn with passion." (1 Corinthians 7:9 ESV) p. 55.

3. Lyrics from the title of "Crooked Deep Down " is a song by Derek Webb, from the album She Must and Shall Go Free released in 2003, p. 59.

4. "Woe to you, scribes and Pharisees, hypocrites! For you are like whitewashed tombs which on the outside appear beautiful, but inside they are full of dead men's bones and all uncleanness." (Matthew 23:27 NASB) p. 60.

5. "The thief comes only to steal and kill and destroy; I have come that they may have life, and have it to the full." (John 10:10, NIV) p. 80.

6. "And when he had removed him, he raised up David to be their king, of whom he testified and said, 'I have found in David the son of Jesse a man after my heart, who will do all my will.'" (Acts 13:22, ESV) p. 82.

7. "When Jesus heard what had happened, he withdrew by boat privately to a solitary place. Hearing of this, the crowds followed him on foot from the towns. When Jesus landed and saw a large crowd, he had compassion on them and healed their sick." (Matthew 14:13–14, NIV) p. 110.

8. Lyrics from the title of "Brushstroke" is a song by Andrew Osenga, from the album Leonard, The Lonely Astronaut released in 2012, p. 160.

9. "But let your 'Yes' be 'Yes,' and your 'No,' 'No.' For whatever is more than these is from the evil one."
(Matthew 5:37, NKJV) p. 180.

10. "And we know that God causes all things to work together for good to those who love God, to those who are called according to His purpose." (Romans 8:28) p. 185.

About the Author

*D*ave is a creative, pastor, and family man. As a writer, photographer, & musician, he's always got a project in his heart, head, and hands. As a pastor, he's concerned with helping people of all walks & situations live a life to the fullest. And as a family man, he's ensuring that all of those he loves become better than he'll ever be. A survivor of a broken home & life-threatening condition, Dave has learned the value and limits of relationships and time. He lives his life in the now, the most important time of all.

Follow along with Dave's adventures
at @fatherinthewild on Instagram.

Visit fatherinthewild.com
to see the pictures and hear the songs from this story.

CPSIA information can be obtained
at www.ICGtesting.com
Printed in the USA
LVHW111224280320
651495LV00001B/7